A Gift *of* Hope

By Danielle Steel

DANIELLE STEEL

A Gift *of* Hope

Helping the Homeless

Delacorte Press ▬ New York

Published in the United States by Delacorte Press,
an imprint of The Random House Publishing Group,
a division of Random House, Inc., New York.

DELACORTE PRESS is a registered trademark of
Random House, Inc., and the colophon is a
trademark of Random House, Inc.

LIBRARY OF CONGRESS CATALOGING-IN-PUBLICATION DATA

Steel, Danielle.
A gift of hope: helping the homeless / Danielle Steel.
p. cm.
ISBN 978-0-345-53136-0 (acid-free paper) —
ISBN 978-0-345-53137-7 (eBook)
1. Homelessness—United States. 2. Homeless persons—
United States. 3. Steel, Danielle. I. Title.
HV4505.S737 2012
362.50973—dc23
2011017260

Printed in the United States of America on acid-free paper

www.bantamdell.com

2 4 6 8 9 7 5 3 1

First Edition

Book design by Virginia Norey

To Nick, who, yet again, has helped so many, even in his absence, for being the guiding light that got me to the streets, and kept me there, for him.

To my wonderful children, Beatrix, Trevor, Todd, Sam, Victoria, Vanessa, Maxx, and Zara, who cheered me on and let me do it, despite the time, expense, and risks.

To Bob, Cody, Jane, Jill, Joe, John, Paul, Randy, Tony, and Younes, for years of hard work, for risking their lives and giving their love and time so generously, and for being the extraordinary people they are. They are the real angels in the story, to me and to so many.

To the many, many wonderful people I have met on the streets, for their kindness, their humanity, their dignity, for allowing us to work among them, and for the privilege of serving them. With the deepest respect, I salute your courage, love, and grace, and thank you for the many gifts you have given me.

To Tom, for urging me to write this, despite all my protests, and for encouraging the street work from the start.

To all of you, with all my heart and love, deep gratitude, and profound respect.

d.s.

And to the memory of Max Leavitt, who was so dearly loved and is so greatly missed.

"Were it not for Hope,
the heart would break."

—*Scottish proverb*

A Gift *of* Hope

FOREWORD

For eleven years, I worked on the streets with the homeless, and without question it altered my life. It is life-changing to be there, to look into the eyes of people who are lost, suffering, sick in body and mind, most of whom have lost hope. They are the forgotten people, whom no one wants to think about or know. For most people it's terrifying to acknowledge them, or see them—what if that could happen to us? It's a horrifying thought. "There but for the grace of God . . ."

I've watched people quietly disintegrate on the streets, and seen some of them go from people without a place to live to people who have no life, no hope, no way out. Some have disappeared, some have died, some of the young ones have gone home, some have gotten help from the available programs and agencies, but most of them are still out there, their situation worsening day by day. And in our fragile economy, the number of people on the streets has increased exponentially.

My goals were never lofty. At first I had no goals at all. In my own grief at having lost a son, I tried to help people who appeared to be in as much pain as I, even if for different reasons. I began to learn what they needed, practically, and to supply those needs. And eventually I realized that my "mission," if you can call it that, was only to keep them alive until real help could address their broader needs. My focus was small and specific: to keep them alive on the streets, to keep them warm and dry and fed, to make them as comfortable as possible in a terrible situation. It was all I could do. I am not a political person, I have no influence on city government, I didn't have enough money to save them all. I'm not a physician or a psychiatrist to address their medical problems. I was one person who wanted to do what I could, with the help of ten others who helped me form what became a very efficient team. We went out night after night, dealt with whatever we found, and served three hundred people a night, three or four thousand a year. We gave them clean, warm new clothing, tools they needed, hygiene supplies, a few practical things like umbrellas and flashlights, pens and pads, and safe, healthy packaged food. And I hope that along the way, we saved a life or two—or more.

Right from the beginning, it was essential to me to remain anonymous in this work, both to the people I served, and in the larger world. I remained convinced that it was completely unimportant who I was. We created something unique, helping to keep the homeless alive on the streets, giving them what they needed most acutely. I felt that my identity was irrelevant and could only get in the way. It didn't matter who I was. Talking about my work on the streets served no purpose either. I was sure that anyone who knew about it would view it with contempt or suspicion, or use it as a springboard to publicity that I didn't want. I wanted to do the work as quietly and invisibly as possible, and I never deviated from that until finally, with what I had learned, I felt that speaking up for them would help them more than my silence.

I am lending the homeless my voice now, so that others will think about them and see their plight. If I, who have walked among them for eleven years and care about them, don't speak for them, who will? Although I have always said that I would never do this, and have done everything I could to stay below the radar, I have finally realized that I need to speak up and share what I've learned. I can be the voice in the world they do not have. There are more people than ever on the streets, there is less and less money available to help them, and some of the laws regarding hospitalization of the mentally ill need to change. But before anything can change, people must be willing to see the homeless and not pretend they aren't there. They so desperately need our help, in so many ways. And we cannot help or change what we refuse to see.

There is so much that needs to be done, and the smallest

effort matters and makes a difference: clothing, meals, medical treatment, psychiatric help, wound care, a ride to an emergency room, a blanket, a kind hand. There is much for even the uninitiated to do. And it takes many to do it.

So this book is a call for help. There are too few of us reaching out to those on the streets, in a silent, unseen war where too many lives are being lost, when in fact so many more could be saved if only people knew, or cared. There are in fact several groups in every city, working diligently to help the homeless in any way they can, and many of them privately organized and funded when city and state governments don't do enough to help.

The homeless need so many things from us. In addition to housing, medical care, mental health care, and job training, they need a strong hand to help them up. And aside from what we can do practically, we need to share our strength and give them hope: the hope that things can change, and the courage to hang on.

I didn't realize it at the time, but along with the supplies we handed out, we gave them hope. We stopped our vans, we jumped out, we walked up to people who had never seen us before and probably wouldn't again, and we handed them bags filled with what they needed to survive for weeks or even months. And we wanted nothing in return. Nothing. They didn't have to embrace our religion, our beliefs, our politics.

They didn't need to know where we came from, or why. They didn't even need to say thank you, although they always did, always. And for one shining instant, they knew with total certainty that someone cared, and fell out of the sky to help them, like an answer to their prayers. It led them to believe that good things could happen again. It showed that someone cared. It gave them hope, which was our most important gift to them.

ONE

How and Why "Yo! Angel!" Started

The homeless outreach team that changed my life, and that of many others, began at a very dark time for me. My son Nick showed signs of suffering from bipolar disease from his earliest childhood. At eighteen months, I found him "different," and precocious long before that (he walked at eight months and spoke in full sentences in two languages when he was a year old). At four, I was convinced that he was manic. When he was five, I sought advice from doctors and psychiatrists who brushed off my concerns, and assured me he was "fine." And when he was seven, I alternated between panic and despair, convinced that he was sick, begging for help for him, while every doctor I consulted reassured me and insisted there was nothing wrong. I have a great fondness now for doctors who respect the bond that mothers have with their children and acknowledge that we know them best of all. I knew my son was sick, but no professional would agree.

When Nick was a very young child, which is not so very long ago, the tradition adhered to by most psychiatrists was that manic depression (or bipolar disease as it is more frequently called now), could not be diagnosed until a patient was in his early twenties, and was staunchly never medicated before that age. The medication most commonly used for bipolar disease was lithium. And it was considered exceptional and almost revolutionary when I found a very respected expert on manic depression at UCLA, who gave Nick lithium at sixteen. And for a brief time, lithium was a miraculous wonder drug for him. For the first time in years he was able to lead what appeared to be a totally normal life because of the drugs, and his diagnosis was established: He was bipolar. To be diagnosed at that age was almost unheard of then. Today, they give lithium to children suspected of being bipolar at four or five. That was unthinkable when Nick was that age. And the belief now is that if you diagnose and medicate bipolar children, they have a much better chance of having a normal life later on.

I've written a whole book about Nick, his illness and his life, his victories and defeats, and our great love for him, so I won't go into detail here. He had two very good years of productive, normal life once he was medicated. And at eighteen, still on the appropriate drugs, he felt so normal that he insisted he wanted to stop taking them. Much to my chagrin (and terror), he spiraled down immediately once off them, and within five weeks he made his first suicide attempt, and very nearly succeeded. Miraculously, he survived, and assured me he wouldn't do it again, but did so ten days later, and was saved again. He made three unsuccessful suicide attempts in three months, then got back on his medications and improved immediately, and with the naïveté of a loving parent, I thought we were home free. After those three suicide attempts, he seemed better, happier, more productive, and more functional than he had ever been, until fierce depression hit him again six months later. He made his final and tragically successful suicide attempt eleven months after the first one, and died at nineteen.

It was a heartbreaking time for me, my eight other children, and all those who knew and loved Nick. Although I have eight wonderful children for whom I am immeasurably grateful, he left an enormous hole in our lives, and will be forever missed. The first months after he died were bleak, to say the least. Like many grieving parents, I had a hard time getting from one day to the next.

To compound things further, as sometimes happens at difficult times, like after a death—particularly the death of a child—my marriage disintegrated as well. Life couldn't have seemed worse. And as the holidays approached, I was in dark despair.

Years before, I had learned a valuable lesson from my oldest daughter, then only fourteen. She had a serious moped accident in our driveway, which damaged her knee, resulting in seven years of grueling physical therapy and repeated surgeries, and kept her on crutches and in wheelchairs for those seven years. It would have been challenging for anyone, and even more so for a young girl of fourteen. She was extremely brave, and in constant pain, and to distract her from her troubles, one of her doctors suggested that she work with people who were even more unfortunate than she. She took the advice to heart, and within a short time she had volunteered in a pediatric cancer ward. And there she found not only something to think about other than her injury, she found her true passion and lifelong vocation. She spent hours there, fell in love with the young patients, volunteered for many years at a summer camp for kids with cancer, and many degrees later, she is a therapist and social worker in a pediatric oncology ward. I can't think of a more heartbreaking job. I admire her immensely for it, and she loves what she does. It is her passion. And I'm sure that in the beginning, at fourteen, it helped keep her mind off her leg and the agony she was in.

During those early days and months after my son's death and the end of my marriage, trying to find some meaning to life and to struggle through such hard times, I went to church every day. I realize that's not for everyone, but it helped get me through it, and to hang on till the next day. And one dark winter evening, I was thinking about what my daughter had done in her teens, reaching out to help people who were in even greater distress than she was, and I prayed about it, kneeling in a dark, candle-lit church. The only things that were keeping me going then were my children and my faith. So with my face in my hands, I prayed for something to make me hold on, and to find a way to help someone else in greater need. The answer came faster than I expected, was loud and clear, and was by no means the answer I wanted. I don't know if I even knew what I hoped the message would be, but surely not the one I got. I didn't like the thought that popped into my head within minutes of my prayer and request for direction and guidance. It came to me very simply: *Help the homeless.* And all I could think was *Oh no!! Not that!! Please!!*

I remained kneeling for a while, and then lit some candles, trying to pretend that I hadn't heard that message clearly in my head. How about some other project? Working with children maybe—I was good at that—or some other nice, neat, clean line of work. All my life I had been a somewhat skittish person, nervous about unusual or ominous-looking people, frightened when drunks or homeless people approached me on the street. It was something I didn't want to see. Their intrusion into my neat, orderly, clean life was something I wanted to avoid, not embrace. But suddenly, in reality, there was no longer perfect order in any aspect of my life anyway. With my son's death and husband's departure, my life was a mess. My life, head, and heart were in disarray. Nick's death had nearly destroyed me, my whole family was badly shaken. Everything had changed.

My children were remarkable to me and one another during that incredibly hard time. There was a sense of solidarity and determined survival, from children who were still so young (five of them from nine to fifteen at the time of their brother's death, and still at home). Although we were very close before Nick's death, it has created an even stronger bond between us since. I remember thinking one night right after he died, as we all gathered for dinner, that we were like survivors of the *Titanic* or some other shipwreck, huddled over our plates, and barely able to speak in our communal pain. And yet we hung on to one another, determined to get through it and one day come to life again. It was a slow and grueling process, with some heavy bumps along the way.

Into that atmosphere of life gone awry, and even despair, came the remarkable message I heard in church: *Help the homeless. Nuts ... no, no ... anything but that.* I resisted the thought with all my might. But I also remembered Nick had always been particularly sensitive to the plight of the homeless.

Whenever he saw a homeless person, he would stop what he was doing, go to the nearest restaurant or food store, and buy them a meal and "a pack of smokes." He would return with his offering, never too busy to take the time to do it. He visited shelters, and as the lead singer of an increasingly successful band, he performed at family shelters whenever he could. So I knew that helping the homeless would have been meaningful to him, which made the voice harder to ignore. But I still didn't like the idea. Not at all!

I had already organized a nonprofit foundation in his name, to assist the mentally ill. But this was different. It was about the homeless. Because the idea had come to me in prayer, the message had a sacred meaning to me and I felt as though I was supposed to follow it, even if I didn't want to. It was close to Christmas, and it seemed like I'd just been given an assignment from "upstairs." I argued with the idea anyway. Wherever the message came from, I spent several more minutes on my knees in church that night, negotiating . . . *come on, God . . . not that . . . how about something else?* No deal. The message kept coming like a subliminal ad: *Help the homeless. Too bad if you don't like it. You asked who to help. I told you. Now go do it.* (I was not thrilled.)

Worse, I had a strange, overwhelming feeling that I had no choice. But believe me, the thought of helping the homeless scared me to death. Being at close range seemed terrifying. I suspect this isn't a unique reaction, since most of us would rather pretend the homeless don't exist. People look through them on the streets, turn away, don't meet their eyes, and whenever possible, would prefer to cross the street to avoid them. Most people would rather leave solving the problem, and ministering to the homeless, to someone else. And to be honest, in my own ignorance that night, so would I. But being a religious person, I figured I had been given a job, and however I felt about it, no matter how reluctant or terrified I was, there was no turning back, no way to act as though I hadn't heard what I did. I was sorry I had asked, as I walked quietly out of church.

I thought about the response to my prayers when I went home that night and the next day, and the day after. But the clear directive wouldn't go away. And finally, I thought, *Okay, God, I get it, I hear you. . . . Okay, I'll do it.* I figured that doing it once would get me off the hook. And hell, I could do anything once. Couldn't I? Yeah, right. So I thought about what to do. I asked a dedicated employee of mine if he'd come out with me on a night just before Christmas, and being a kind person, he agreed. I bought warm down jackets, a stack of sleeping bags, and some wool socks and gloves. I can't remember how many, probably around forty or fifty of each. We put it all in a van, and set out on a bitter cold night. And I will admit that I was gritting my teeth, but there was something of an adrenaline rush too. I don't think it was excitement as much as fear. I had no idea who or what we would encounter, nor what to expect, and I was anxious to fulfill my mission, do the job, and get it over with. Nothing in the message I'd heard said I had to do it more than once.

I remembered a few homeless people I had seen in regular spots in doorways in my neighborhood, so we stopped there first. People were already tucked in for the night by the time we went out, shielded behind pieces of cardboard boxes and staying warm as best they could. And the reaction we got, each time we stopped, was one of surprise, and instant gratitude. Suddenly, their faces lit up, as clean, new, good-quality sleeping bags were put into their hands; warm jackets were handed out and immediately put on and zipped up; gloves went onto hands; and people took off battered shoes and put on warm socks. And as I looked at them, met their eyes, and touched their hands, I was no longer scared, but deeply humbled by their warmth and humanity. I was suddenly embarrassed by the fearful thoughts I had had about them for years. Other than the births of my children, it was probably one of the most important nights of my life.

I had already learned a hard lesson, that no matter how "comfortable" we are in life, whatever our "station" or "rank" appears to be, however "safe" we want to believe ourselves, we aren't. We are right out there in the front row of life's storms, whoever we are, and whatever we have. I had lost my so-much-beloved, precious son, my sweet boy, and then a husband whom I also loved. I had learned firsthand that tragedy and disappointment can strike any of us at any time. For me, right then, it didn't get worse than that. Other things happen to people—catastrophic illness, tragedies, whole families die in fires whether you are rich or poor, road accidents claim high school students who have families who love them—and these people I was handing sleeping bags to had wound up on the streets. So how safe are any of us? We just aren't. Bad things happen to good people all the time. The phrase "There but for the grace of God go I" never seemed truer to me than that night. And as we handed out sleeping bags and jackets, I couldn't help thinking how proud Nick would have been of me—I who had so often shrunk beside him when he reached out to some homeless person with a hot meal, who had pursed my lips and told him he shouldn't hug them because he might get a disease. God forgive me. What a different world I walked into that night.

After we had delivered our goods to the people I knew where to find, we began driving, drifting from the safe familiarity of the neighborhood I lived in, crossing invisible borders into uncharted land and some dicier neighborhoods. And the people I was looking for were painfully easy to find: in doorways, in parking lots, in dark alleys, sometimes in little clusters of five or six, sometimes in pairs, sometimes alone, always startled and unable to comprehend what was happening. Why were we giving them things they needed desperately? What was it all about? We represented no church, no organization, no religion, no agency, no shelter. We wanted nothing from them. We just stopped and asked if they needed what we had to give, and, without exception, they did. Some laughed, some cried, some hugged us, and every single person said the exact same thing as we left: "Thank you. And God bless you." Every single one. I was impressed by their kindness, decency, and good manners. I couldn't think of the last time anyone had said "God bless you" to me, even in church.

Once or twice, with my eyes held by theirs, I whispered, "Please say a prayer for a boy called Nick," feeling embarrassed to ask them even for that, but the words came out on their own. How often had he fed them and sung for them in shelters—maybe they could say a little prayer for him now. Maybe it would help. He had been gone for exactly three months.

I asked no questions of the people I met that night, nor in the years after. Others are curious about how they wound up on the streets. Was it bad luck, bad management of their income, drink, drugs, a broken marriage, a lost job, or an illness? All of the above? I never knew, and I believed I had no right to ask. Eventually, I made some fairly accurate guesses, knowing the streets better, and some people volunteered their stories. But I always felt (and still do) that privacy was the last shred of dignity they had. They didn't have to tell me what happened in order to earn what I had to give. I gave my heart and respect along with the supplies. They didn't have to give me anything back, and surely not the stories of their lives, which belonged only to them. Did we see signs of drink or drugs that first night? Some. Did some look mentally ill? Yes, many in fact. But living on the street in winter conditions, with no hope of getting off the street, who knows what any of us would do to survive? And for those who are mentally ill and should be on medication they can't afford and don't have access to, alcohol and street drugs are the only available form of self-medication to dull the pain of their lives.

Did I have a sense of danger? No. Were there signs of violence or any threats to us? No. People were cold, shivering, frozen, but above all grateful and always kind. On that first night, we went into less fortunate neighborhoods, but we didn't venture into the really dangerous areas where we would make our rounds later on. That night was our christening on the streets, and it was a gentle one. The employee I had brought with me was as impressed as I. And since we had no idea what we were doing or how to do it, our end of the operation was more than a little haphazard.

We had stacks of jackets (in one size, large, I think) piled up in the back of the van. We had sleeping bags thrown every-where, and were constantly digging for a matching glove or sock. We would emerge with our offerings loose in our arms, hand them over, and move on to the next stop. There was nothing smooth about it—all it was, at our end, was a pile of "stuff" and a lot of heart. And as far as we were concerned, the night was going well. What we gave them was absorbed into doorways and alleys in about an hour. There were so many people in dire need that we could have given away hundreds of sleeping bags and jackets that night if we had them. Giving away forty or fifty jackets and sleeping bags was like empty-ing the ocean with a thimble. I have never felt so small and insignificant in my life.

It was hard to come face-to-face with such acute need and misery, and feel so helpless. It dug deep into one's heart, mine for sure. I thought it was going to be a single, extraordinary experience for me, and I was both touched and in somewhat good spirits. In many ways, it was the best night I had had in a long time, and certainly the most useful one. And predictably, for a short time at least, it took my mind off my troubles. These people were, without question, far worse off than I. So the mission, that cold December night, was a success. I felt as though I'd done the right thing, and heeded the message I'd heard. And I thought I only "had" to do it once.

But as I later discovered, and as happened every time we

went out over the years, God threw us The Big One, the curve ball, at the last stop. He always did. It never failed in eleven years after that. We stopped on the way back to my house, in front of a bank. We saw two piles of "things": boxes, a blanket, what looks like debris until you realize it's someone's house, or "crib," as they're called on the street. One of the men who joined us to do this work shortly after, and is one of the founding members of the group, used to see cribs like these, and cheerfully call out "table for two!" so we would know how many to prepare for. In any case, we were aware that we were stopping for two people, and thus far it had been a good night.

As we approached the doorway to the bank, which was somewhat sheltered, we saw only one person, or form, between the two piles of stuff. I couldn't see the sex or age of the person, who was lying on a single piece of cardboard, with a thin, tattered blanket covering the form. A wheelchair caught my eye at the edge of the small encampment, and I assumed we would be meeting an old woman or man. We called out, asking if the person needed a sleeping bag or a warm jacket, and a young woman sat up and looked me in the eye. She was beautiful, with a face like an angel, long blond hair, neatly brushed, and huge blue eyes. She looked at me, frightened at first, and we explained that we had some warm jackets, sleeping bags, gloves, and socks to give away. In fact, we only had two sets left, and had been careful not to stop at larger groups on the way back, so as not to disappoint anyone or cause a fight. So this was definitely our last stop.

"You're giving them away?" she said, looking stunned. I nodded and smiled, as her face dissolved before me and she started to cry. She couldn't say anything, she just sat there on the street sobbing, shivering in the cold, and she thanked us profusely when she caught her breath. She said that she was with her mother, who had gone to use the bathroom at a nearby McDonald's and would be back in a minute. We went to the van, and got what we had left, as I wished it was more. And when we came back, she volunteered that she was twenty-one, had cancer, had just started chemotherapy, and was starting to lose her hair. My stomach turned over as I listened. She could have been one of my older children. How could she be living on the street, covered by one ragged blanket and undergoing chemo? She kept thanking us and crying, unable to believe that we had appeared in the night and had anything to give her. As we talked, her mother returned, and the four of us chatted. They said they were afraid to go to a shelter, and had gotten hurt in shelters before. (Rapes, robberies, and muggings are common in homeless shelters.) They said they would rather take their chances on the streets, where they felt safer, than risk violence in a shelter. They quickly put on the jackets and got into the sleeping bags, and after talking a little more, feeling helpless, we wished them good things. They thanked and blessed us when we left.

Back in the van, we were silent for the ride back to my house. Not a word was said. My mind was full of all we had seen, and my heart was aching for that beautiful and very sick young girl. I was haunted by her face, and everything she had said. And I did not know it yet, as I climbed out of the empty van back at my house, but that last stop had done it. The twenty-one-year-old girl with cancer had ripped out my heart. God's Last-Stop Curve Ball had hit me squarely in the gut. I was hooked.

TWO

Second Night Out

The night after our venture out to "help the homeless" (What help? A few jackets and some sleeping bags? In the face of all they needed, who was kidding whom?) was the night of my annual Christmas party, which for twenty years had been a lavish event. It was a different time, when the economy was stable and the world wasn't as austere as it is now. That night, I had a hundred people in black tie for dinner, including well-known socialites, a smattering of famous people, the mayor, some other politicians, a congresswoman, a senator, and several judges. Although my daily life was spent at the orthodontist or soccer games, and driving carpools—the life of the mother of nine kids—my parties had always been a big deal, and I went all out. I had debated canceling that year, because of my son, but decided it would be even more depressing for me and my children to sit in a dark house and not follow familiar traditions or see friends. So I gave the same party I did every year. I wore a long black evening gown, and the guests were well dressed and bejeweled. There was a band. People danced. There's no question it was beautiful, even if I wasn't having a good time. And the reality was, my wearing sackcloth and ashes wasn't going to change the plight of people on the street. And my interest in the homeless was very new to me. So the show went on. What was different was that, as I sat at my dinner party, I felt like I was crawling out of my skin. I was nervous, distracted, haunted by all that we had seen the night before, and particularly the young woman and her mother at our last stop. I could think of nothing else.

I was seated next to a high-up elected city official, and I casually brought up the issue of the homeless in the city and their seemingly growing numbers. He complained somewhat irascibly that people who try to help them don't know what they're doing and only make things worse. The more you give them, he insisted, the longer they'll dig in their heels and stay on the street. It seemed a strange theory to me. Why would anyone *want* to stay on the street for a sleeping bag and a pair of socks? It made no sense to me (and still doesn't, although it is the excuse most often used for people doing nothing to help). The subject changed. The night went on. The mayor and I danced a time or two. And at last everyone went home. By then, I wasn't crawling out of my skin, I knew exactly what

I wanted to do. I just hoped I could find them again, at the bank.

The employee who had helped me the night before was also working that night. He looked very different in black tie than he had the night before. As soon as the guests left, I told him my plan, and his eyes lit up as he agreed to join me in a quick visit to the streets. I rushed upstairs, took my dress off, and climbed into jeans, boots, a wool cap, a sweater, and a ski parka. He changed into jeans and a warm jacket too. And five minutes later we drove off in the van. I had a moment of feeling like Robin Hood, one minute dancing with the mayor, the next driving off in the dark of night. And much to my chagrin, when we got to the bank, the young woman with cancer and her mother were gone. Damn. It had seemed like such a good idea, but got us nowhere. For the next hour, we drove around. I didn't want to go home until we found them. I couldn't bear thinking of that sick girl and her mother on the street.

Finally, we found them in the dark recesses of a nearby parking lot, tucked away in a corner. The gleam of the wheelchair had caught our eye. I gently woke them up and we offered to give them a ride to a shelter, which they refused, and I gave them enough money for a hotel for a week. They said they knew of one where they could stay. There was more crying, more hugging, more blessings, and more thanks. We gave them our cell phone numbers and asked them to let us know how they were. They were the only homeless people I ever gave my phone number to, or gave money to.

What followed, over long months, were several visits with them on the street, and many phone calls. I got them into a women's shelter twice and they wouldn't stay. We followed them for close to a year, maybe longer, unable to really provide any solid long-term help, just the knowledge that someone cared. They always bounced right back onto the street—the mother was feisty and didn't comply well with shelter rules. Eventually, we learned that the young woman had died. I could never find her mother after that, she vanished from the streets. I don't know what happened to her, but that young woman with her lovely face and gentle ways got me hooked for all those years on the streets. I never forgot her and never will. Many faces and many people since then have snagged my heart and stuck in my mind, but that one young girl was special to me. I only wish I could have made more difference than I did. The only thing we could do was show her that someone cared. It was all we had to give. And for as long as we could, we tried to give her hope. But she and her mother were typical of many who feel more at home living on the streets, despite bad weather, bad people, and bad times. To many, shelters, where violence, petty crimes, and disease abound, seem more dangerous. They have more friends and feel safer on the streets. For others, long-sought-after housing isolates them when they finally get it. Once alone in an apartment, they fall prey to depression, and far too often suicide is the result. Although the risks and discomforts on the street are obvious, for many homeless people it is a comfortable, familiar world.

After our second meeting with the young woman and her mother, I felt that I had done my job and fulfilled my mission. But something had changed in my life during those two nights, a piece of me had shifted, and I was forever different. You don't go back to who you were before. You are never, ever the same again. It is permanently life-altering to discover the world on the streets. But I didn't know that at the time.

I thought then that I was off the hook. The message I'd heard didn't tell me to make a career of it, it just said to go do it, and I did. So I went back to my daily doings and ordinary life, working and being with my kids. I had no plan to do it again. And then a week later, right before Christmas, I heard *Go back and do it again.* Nuts! I was less reluctant than the first time, but I'll admit, I dragged my feet a bit. And then finally, I gave in. *Okay, okay, I'm going. Yeesh.* Sometimes God is a little pushy, and even pushes hard. He did.

This time I asked two employees and two friends to join me, and we filled the van until it was bursting. We even had jackets in two sizes. And as we drove out that cold night, in a driving rain, I was not quite sure that this would be our last visit to the streets, nor that I wanted it to be.

John and Jane, the couple who joined me that second time, were the perfect choice. They were close friends of mine and had done years of hands-on work for a variety of causes, most recently taking care of people with AIDS, bringing them meals and comfort. The misery of the human condition is no surprise to them, and they were anxious to join me in reaching out to the homeless. They were the only people I confided in about what I was doing. Right from the beginning, and not even sure why, I had a strong sense that this was something I didn't want to talk about, or share with people I knew. I had always had a powerful belief that good deeds should be done anonymously and in silence. They lose meaning when you toot your own horn, expect acknowledgment or praise, or talk about them. It has taken me more than a dozen years to break that silence, which I've done only because I felt that the homeless could be best served by waking people up and sharing what I've seen.

John and Jane have huge hearts, willing hands, strong backs, and are full of creativity and spirit. An artist with tremendous talent, Jane also spent years working in retail, and jumped excitedly into ordering what we needed when I shared this project with her. John, a professor at a major university, has a profound love for young people, anyone in need, and is always willing to help.

On that second trip into the streets, we still had no idea what we were doing. Once again jackets were piled all over the place, sleeping bags were jammed everywhere, and boxes of gloves and socks were spilling onto the van floor. Our hearts were in the right place, and wide open, and we had no idea who we would meet or what we would find. I had no sense yet of who exactly lived on the streets, and no precise idea of what they needed. All I knew was that they were cold and wet, and anything we could bring them would be an improvement. I realized that they must be hungry too, but offering food as well as sleeping bags and warm jackets seemed way too complicated to me. So we stuck to the initial concept of sleeping bags, jackets, socks, and gloves. For now, it seemed like the best we could do.

We set off in anticipation of the night, excited about it, chatting animatedly. It was cold and rainy. I was wearing foul-weather gear that I had used in boating. I must have looked like a large yellow rubber duck in overalls, hooded jacket, and rubber boots. The others wore similar gear, but whatever we were wearing, by our second or third stop we were soaking wet. In a rain that was blowing sideways in a strong wind, there seemed to be no way to stay dry that night. And if we were cold and damp in our foul-weather gear, the condition of the people we stopped for was beyond belief. Some were in T-shirts plastered to their skin in the rain, jeans that were soaked, and shoes that were dissolving. Many had bare feet, and everyone was shivering, many sick, coughing or with fevers. Few had jackets, and they must have looked at us like we were from outer space, particularly me in my ridiculous rubber-ducky yellow suit.

Our good humor and good spirits, and nervously exchanged bad jokes between stops, began to dissipate as the night wore on. What we were seeing was just too hard, and basically too sad. The people we stopped for were so cold, miserable, and too often sick. Women were crying, men looked dazed. We wanted to put our arms around them, instead of just jackets. Our offerings seemed so meager, and their plight so extreme. And worse yet, it was almost Christmas. Understandably, the holiday seemed not to matter on the streets. No one had mentioned it all night.

I would love to offer humor from that night, to lighten the mood, but there was so little of it. There was plenty of laughter in the van, at the beginning of the evening, mostly out of nervousness, I think. We were out of our element, in an unfamiliar world even in our own city, and sometimes when you're scared, it's easier to be funny than to admit to grief. But there was nothing funny as the night wore on, nothing to laugh at. It was all so touching, so raw, and so poignant. It raked my heart over barbed wire, and I left a piece of myself forever on those streets.

That night, I stood over an old man sleeping on church steps in the pouring rain, and gently woke him. I was carrying a jacket I hoped was his size, and a rolled-up sleeping bag under my arm. As he woke, he looked at me through dim eyes, and more than likely he'd been drinking (maybe the only way he had to keep warm, or at least blot out the reality of how he was living). He blinked as he looked up at me, unable to comprehend what he was seeing. "Did I die?" he asked, with an air of amazement.

"No, no," I reassured him, and handed him a down jacket and sleeping bag. He was still staring as I ran back down the steps to join the others. He called out his thanks and blessed me, and as I turned back to wave, I saw him struggling into the jacket, and then unrolling the sleeping bag, shaking his head.

We had no sense of mission then, and I don't think any of us could have named or labeled it at that point. That came a long time later. Those first nights were "one-night stands," something we felt led to do, with no thought beyond those moments. We went into some of the rougher parts of town that night but had no sense of danger. People were too cold, too wet, and too miserable to present any threat to us. Later, much later, we learned that although miserable, the cold, hard, wet nights were safest for us. When people are deeply engaged in their own survival, there is rarely a thought of harming others. Sometimes on warmer, easier nights, on the streets there is an almost tangible tension, a sense of people looking for trouble, angry at what is happening to them, which created stressful moments for us too. Longer days in summer months were more dangerous for us, when we could be plainly seen from a great distance by those who were occasionally less well meaning, or preyed on others. We worked best, and in the safest conditions, in darkness and in bad weather. Hard for us, and for the homeless, but less risky for the team.

But on that second night, there was no danger, just a lot of cold, acutely uncomfortable people. The jackets and sleeping bags helped, but surely not enough. I was discovering at each stop that our showing up brought more than just warm, dry gear, it brought the message that people who didn't know them and wanted nothing from them cared enough to find them and bring something they needed. Maybe we could have just as easily brought cardboard boxes or orange crates or old galoshes. The idea that someone had come out in the pouring rain, and gave a damn, was a powerful message. The gift we shared that night was one of hope, which was an important theme for us too. If someone could show up unexpectedly and without motive—why couldn't it happen to us in our own lives, bringing us what we needed? It was a gift like no other, and I realized then that what was happening was just as important for us as it was for them. Who doesn't need hope in their lives: hope that something can change, that someone cares, that not only bad things happen unexpectedly but good things can happen to us too?

At one of our last stops, a huge man, who might have frightened me if I'd been alone on a dark street with him, broke into a smile that was dazzling. He looked into the sky with the most beautiful teeth and grin I'd ever seen, and laughed out loud. "Thank YOU, GOD!" he shouted heavenward, echoing what was in my heart. And of course, he thanked us too, and blessed us as we left.

Everywhere we went, people asked us where we came from, what church, what group, what organization. The answer was always "nowhere," that we were just a group of friends who wanted to do this. There was no way to tell them why, we didn't know ourselves, except for the message I'd heard in church, which sounded weird even to me. (I didn't tell anyone about that.) The people we handed sleeping bags and jackets to were surprised, and mystified, but also grateful and pleased.

And this trip, with more jackets, sleeping bags, and people in the van than the first time, our supplies were a mess after a few stops. Socks and gloves were everywhere, sleeping bags rolled out of the van, fortunately in plastic covers, and the down jackets slid all over the place—having two sizes made sense but made it more confusing. We were constantly shouting to each other, "Socks, I need SOCKS!" "I can't find the large jackets" "Give me a medium. . . . a MEDIUM!" for some tiny, shivering woman. It was painfully haphazard, albeit well intentioned, not sloppy so much as chaotic. Eventually we found what we needed, but we were running all over each other, trying to make sure that each person had one of everything, and we ran out of supplies all too quickly. I was stunned, yet again, at how rapidly we used up what we'd brought, with so many people left who needed everything.

That night, we had enough for seventy-five people, and I doubt that what we had lasted two hours. Suddenly the van was empty, there were no sleeping bags rolling out of it, no more jackets to offer, no socks, no gloves. Much too quickly, we had nothing left to give. I always hated the part of the night when you had to drive home, trying not to see the people in doorways that we hadn't been able to get to. It was painful beyond words, and sometimes we cried as we drove past them. I went home at night thinking not only of those we had met and supplied, but, with an aching heart, of those we hadn't, and sometimes thinking of them more than the others. Emptying the ocean with a thimble again, our thimbles so tiny, and the ocean of need so huge.

Interestingly, and contrary to what most people would expect, no one asked us for money. The question was never raised. In eleven years on the streets, I was asked for money once, and then only for a dollar. People were so grateful for what we had to give, and so respectful, that I don't think it even occurred to them to ask for more. Once in a while, people would ask for a cigarette, but rarely. They were thrilled with what they did get, and deeply thankful. They had learned to expect nothing from life, and so many had lost hope, that a gift of any kind was a wondrous thing. They taught me much about gratitude, for what one has or is given, without wishing for anything more.

Our little team worked well that night. More than any of us, Jane kept tabs on what we had in the van and gave us a running count of what was left as our supplies disappeared into the streets. Concerned about not having enough for everyone, we were careful not to stop at groups that were too big for us. The last thing we wanted was to disappoint or upset people, and we also didn't want to risk their anger or frustration. Jane kept us on track, and seemed to have a hundred hands as she pulled what we needed from the back of the van, sometimes climbing into and over the supplies herself, a loving octopus in gym shoes. And John, with his deeply compassionate face and kind eyes, looked at people in a way that left no doubt how much he cared about them. It was as though he had waited his whole life to meet each of them, and people responded immediately to him. Tony, one of my two employees with us, spoke to people we met in Spanish when necessary, and was unfailingly cheerful and upbeat as he handed out supplies. Younes, who had been with me on the first night, drove us patiently from one stop to the next, and his gentleness and size alone were impressive to watch, and kept us safe on the streets wherever we ventured. And although only in spirit, my son Nick was with us that night too. I thought about him a lot, and wanted him to be part of this event in some tangible way, since indirectly he had caused it to happen. I had put his watch on at the last minute, right before we went out. It comforted me to see it on my wrist, and made him seem part of the action in a real way. I always wear his ring. And since that night, I have always worn Nick's watch when on the streets. It has kept him with us, and with me.

All in all, it was a good night, even if a wet and hard one. There were faces and moments we all remembered and took with us as we drove home. We had one set of supplies left in the back of the van but had seen no singles in a while. We were keeping an eye out for one. And then, of course, it came, God's famous Last-Stop Curve Ball. Like the girl with cancer I had met on the first night, this last person nearly did me in. I saw him out of the corner of my eye, and we nearly drove past him. He was sitting in a doorway in an alley, a single figure, perfect for the one outfit we had left. I called out to stop the van, which Younes did, we got out, and I walked toward a young man. I don't know why, but I knew that this boy was meant for me, and even now I cry as I write about him. As we approached, I could see how young he was. He had long hair and a youthful face, and he was soaked to the skin. He was blond, and he had a face like Jesus. He had sores all over his face, and inevitably I thought of AIDS, but I was not really thinking as I looked at him, I was feeling. He was mumbling incoherently, and his blue eyes seemed to look through me. He looked to be about nineteen or twenty, the same age as Nick.

He was just a boy, sitting on a doorstep, soaking wet, in a shirt and jeans. He had one leg, the other was amputated at the knee, and his crutches were scattered on the street around him. I walked to him, momentarily speechless, unable to even offer him what we had to give. I stood there with tears rolling down my cheeks as he spoke deliriously. And then finally I was able to tell him that we had a warm jacket and a sleeping bag for him. He nodded. I offered to take him somewhere but he shook his head vehemently. For a moment, I almost wondered if my mind was playing some kind of trick. Was I seeing this only so that I would know how badly we were needed? And if Nick hadn't been so lovingly cared for all his life, is this how he would have wound up, with one leg, delirious, soaking wet on the streets? This boy was clearly the same age, and seemed possibly mentally ill. And as much as I reached out to that boy that night, I knew I was also doing it for his mother. Would some other woman have done that for me, if it had been Nick? One could only hope so.

I set our supplies down on the step next to him and stood there for a long moment, as slowly he pulled himself back into the doorway, a little more out of the rain, and we stayed there looking at each other. I said, "God bless you," because I didn't know what else to say, and it took all my strength to turn around and walk away, to leave him there and not put my arms around him. I was still crying when I got back to the van, and no one spoke on the way home. There was not a sound.

Unlike others, whom I sometimes ran into repeatedly over the years, I never saw that boy again. It's hard to believe he's still alive, given the condition he was in that night. It made me grateful Nick had never come to that, and it made me realize again how lucky we had been to have him, even if we lost him too soon. I tucked that boy in the doorway into my heart that night, and I will carry him there forever.

THREE

The Team

With the second night on the streets, I supposed I had fulfilled my mission. I had listened to the message in church, followed directions, and gone out there. Twice. Three times, if you counted the time I went back to see the girl with cancer after my Christmas party. But by January, I knew it wasn't a one- or two-time thing.

I remembered nearly every face we had seen so far, and I had become aware of a need so enormous that there was no way I could turn my back on it. I had seen too much to pretend it wasn't happening, in my own backyard, in my own city.

There were other things I could have done, like work through an established organization. I knew of a family shelter, and had sent them gifts at Christmas. There are two incredibly efficient dining rooms for the homeless in San

Francisco. But the idea of going to work for some organization already established to help the homeless didn't appeal to me. I wanted to continue what we'd started. And even if it was uncomfortable and unnerving at times, even scary, I liked working outdoors, on the streets, going out to look for people, and handing them things directly. That way, I knew they received what we intended to give them, and I wasn't relying on others to distribute what we had bought.

I had a strong sense that those who were in the most dire need, or the least functional, were not able to find their way to dining rooms, churches, or shelters. I wanted to go to them and find them where they were. And it seemed to me that if I was going to do that, I needed to think it out, and approach the project with a certain degree of order. I spoke to Jane about it, and we decided to order jackets in three sizes for men—medium, large, and extra large—because we had been aware that some of our larges were too small for big men we met on the streets. But our mediums were often too big for women. There were far more men on the streets, maybe ten men to one woman, but there were enough women out there, we thought, to justify ordering jackets in two sizes for them. Likewise, we ordered socks in two sizes. We stuck with the gloves, and decided to add wool beanies. Our inventory was growing. We decided to go all out and order a hundred of everything for our next trip out.

We also realized that we needed a team if we were going to do this regularly. It had been a lot of work for just five of us, jumping in and out of the van all night, and there were safety issues to think of also. There were two policemen I knew well, and I called them to ask if they'd be willing to do this with us when off duty. My one condition in every case was that they tell no one, and they agreed.

Randy and Bob, the two policemen, instantly enlisted. I didn't know how often we would go out on our secret missions, but I knew I wanted to go back into the streets again, maybe on a regular basis. Eventually, we decided to go once a month, in two vans. It took that long to stock up and reorder things, and even in the beginning, the project was expensive. I decided it was something I wanted to underwrite, and how I wanted to spend my money.

We all noticed that each time we went out, there was a unique atmosphere to the evening. No two trips were the same. Ever. The weather affected the spirits of the people we met, but aside from that, there was a different mood on the streets on any given night. Sometimes it was more serious, almost gloomy, at other times somber, or there would be a strange aura of tension that seemed ominous to all of us. At other times people were more lighthearted, less tense, and easy, and even joked with us for a minute. Sometimes we glided through the evenings without a hitch. At other times we felt frightened and more worried for our safety, and could feel a palpable tension. It was impossible to predict, but the atmosphere on the streets seemed to have a life of its own.

That unpredictable aura we were all aware of made it even more important to have the right team.

In addition to Tony and Younes, and Bob and Randy, the two off-duty policemen, two more of my employees were enthusiastic about signing up. Cody and Paul had both been Nick's nurses, and had gone to work in other ways in my office after his death, Paul in security, and Cody as an executive assistant who helped run the foundation we had set up in Nick's memory. Although I never said so openly, they both sensed correctly that this homeless work had a lot to do with Nick, and both men wanted to be involved. John and Jane were still enthusiastic participants. That brought our team up to nine. Knowing the terminology now, which I didn't then, we became an "outreach team," reaching out to people on the streets. Other outreach teams working on the streets do different things, but none did exactly what we did, offering warm clothing and sleeping bags to the people we served.

There was very little coordination or even communication among the other outreach teams we encountered, and often they didn't even know about one another. Each group was operating independently and doing what they could. And there seemed to be no overlap of services. We had each found a niche and a role we were good at. And the homeless needed us all.

So that was our original team: Younes, Tony, Paul, Cody, Bob, Randy, Jane, John, and me. That seemed like plenty to us. Later we were joined by two more off-duty police officers who were also friends, Jill and Joe. And much later, on a few rare occasions, I took close friends into my confidence and invited them out with me. They were stunned by what they saw, and I swore them to secrecy about what I was by then doing on a regular basis.

But in the beginning we were a team of nine. We realized that with nine of us, and supplies for a hundred people, we needed more than the two vans we were using. I still had Nick's van in the garage, the one he had used to tour with his band. It was covered inside and out with graffiti and stickers from a variety of bands they had toured or played with, and it was pure Nick. I loved the idea of using his van. It was another way of making him part of our experiences, and a sweet memory of him as we drove around.

The safety of the team was very important to me. I was very grateful that no one had gotten hurt so far (and thankfully never did). We always reminded one another to be cautious if someone on the team got too relaxed and less alert (usually me). It was also risky business to take the uninitiated out with us, and we avoided it most of the time. We worked in dangerous areas, serving unpredictable people. Lack of awareness, a moment's hesitation, stopping to ask "why" instead of getting out fast if we had to, could put all of us at risk, and it was more comfortable to work with people who knew what they were doing. And we, as a team, were slowly gaining experience and becoming more savvy.

Among the few who joined us to lend a spare pair of hands hauling bags out of the van was a dear friend, Michael, who is a person of deep religious leanings. Like Jane and John, he had worked for many years with people with AIDS, through hospice. And after his work with us, he went to the Middle East, Liberia, and South America as a missionary. He was wonderful doing outreach on the streets and became a frequent member of our team. As we began to serve more people, our operation went more smoothly if there were twelve or thirteen of us. It distributed the work better and kept us safer, so we were willing to take one or two additional people with us, if they seemed suitable.

Eleven on the team were barely enough and more than thirteen were too many. But adding the wrong "guest worker" was more headache than it was worth. Although our nighttime activities sounded appealing to compassionate people, coming face-to-face with the hard physical work of unloading the vans, carrying the supplies, and confronting the dangers on the streets and miserable conditions in bad weather scared most people off, and they didn't sign up again. It was never what they expected and was always hard to predict or describe beforehand—and some nights were tougher than others. The risks we faced, became used to, and took as commonplace were frightening to people who had never been out there before. For some it was just too much. Others found it remarkable, but had no desire to join us again. We always understood and were grateful for their help, even once.

When we began our work, we used two vans and eventually added Nick's as a third. Seeing his van always gave me the comforting sensation that Nick was with us. And halfway through the night, we would reload the third van (which left us short-handed temporarily and was a little dicey for the rest of us). But we delivered four vanloads of goods to the streets, and the system of reloading worked. Using trucks would have been too cumbersome. And four vanloads of goods were all we could afford. If we had had the funds to do it, we could have given away twice as much—the need was always there.

As our outreach team grew in the beginning, we formed a group of volunteers to sort and pack the supplies. It took two or three weekends to do it, with Jane overseeing and ordering the supplies. With time, we became increasingly organized.

We left for our "missions" shortly after six o'clock at night, with the vans loaded. We realized that going at night made the most sense, because in the daytime people on the streets roam around, pushing carts and wandering. It was easier to locate them once they settled down for the night, so we went out after dark, and it was safer for us to go out when we were less visible.

I always prayed silently for the safety of everyone involved. Despite my enthusiasm and commitment to the idea, I was well aware, as we all were, that there were dangers on the streets, and obvious risks. We had no set plan as to how to deal with those dangers, but two things gave me the illusion that we were safe. One was that the idea had come to me in church. How could anything happen to us if we were sent out there to do God's work? I mentioned this to a priest once, who was quick to respond that the church does not canonize the foolish. Good point. And it took me a while to realize that getting the idea in church did not guarantee our safe passage on the streets, not by any means. We had some close calls over the years. You have to watch your back, be smart, alert, and sometimes get out of the way fast.

I was reassured by the presence of four off-duty police who were part of our group. But even that didn't guarantee that we would have no mishaps, I realized later, because we spread out, we found ourselves at times alone with groups of home-less people around us in dangerous neighborhoods and situa-

A Gift of Hope

tions, and bad things can happen fast. But certainly having police officers with us helped, and I might not have been brave enough to do it otherwise long-term. I was concerned with the well-being of everyone on the team. Our police officers in the group never had to put their professional skills to use, but their awareness, caution, instincts, and expertise at handling difficult situations saved us more than once, and probably avoided greater problems.

More than once, as we set out for the night's work, I remembered a film I had seen as a child about bullfighters, and how they prayed before going into the ring. Strangely, I felt like that, not sure what we'd be facing, but praying that everyone would come back unhurt and alive. I felt very responsible for the team. Going to mass before our nights on the streets became a ritual for me, as well as lighting candles for everyone working. No matter how comfortable I got out there, I never lost sight of the risks or the potential dangers of what we were doing, and that we were on the streets with the grace of God, and hopefully doing His work as best we could.

No one ever had time to eat before we took off in the vans, so someone had once thought to bring a big box of doughnuts. They became the source of many jokes over the years, but they actually sustained us through the night. Later, trying to add a more "upscale" note, Bob brought a box of almond croissants. These two items became traditions on our trips.

Unfortunately, both boxes always sat next to me in the van, and I ate far too many of them every time, but they really hit the spot! It was a crazy diet for nights when we needed a lot of energy, but it was all any of us ever ate on those nights, along with occasional offerings of popcorn from Jill. Most of the time, we were too excited, and running on too much adrenaline, to eat. If thirsty, we drank soda or water. We never stopped for coffee, even when we were cold. We didn't want to slow down, stop, or waste time. We had better things to do.

Each time we did outreach, we headed south, three vans in convoy, past a small park where homeless people camp on the grass, even in cold weather. There was no shelter there, but there was a lot of space, and a church across the street, with a handful of people in the doorway. This became our traditional first stop of the night, and most of the time, with rare exceptions, we did a lot of "business" there. We were still giving away loose goods in the beginning, and Jane had organized them well, each size in separate boxes, each item readily available, and one of the vans with only sleeping bags. With three sizes of jackets for men and two for women, my first question as I walked up to people, after telling them we had things for them, was "Excuse me, sir, are you a large or an extra large?" The men stared at me as though I was crazy, and the team made fun of me. (After a while, I could pretty much eyeball our clients and guess the right size.) There was a lot of teasing among the team about our "winter line" as opposed to our "spring line," and if someone would be coming out to do alterations later. It kept the mood light in the early part of the evening, when we were able to give people items that really fit in the correct size.

With off-duty cops on board, we were braver about venturing into some nasty neighborhoods that night, and thereafter. We felt a confidence that maybe we shouldn't have, but we wanted to be where we were needed most. And the policemen added fearlessness. They knew what they were doing and what not to confront. We made some early safety rules, and set some boundaries about neighborhoods. There were so many homeless people in the city that there were a lot of options. We decided to avoid the Panhandle area of Garden Gate Park, near the once-famous Haight-Ashbury, because there were mostly transient young people there, almost all of whom were high on drugs, and whose homelessness often stemmed from that. We wanted to get to the hardcore homeless at the bottom of the barrel, where no one else would go, not the "cream" at the top.

Our fear was that in the Panhandle, the kids would be most likely to sell what we gave them, for more drugs, which seemed to defeat our purpose. There were also parts of the

park where our police teammates felt it was just too dangerous for us to go, where we would have to climb through
bushes in the dark and were too likely to get attacked. Likewise, we made Hunter's Point off limits, where street violence
was extreme and where shootings occurred too frequently
for our safety. We eliminated another area where dirty nee-
dles were the weapon of choice. And the police on our team
said that if we worked in the Tenderloin, we were likely to inadvertently interrupt the flow of business in drug traffic, and
we were liable to get killed. Sixth Street was the hotbed of
drug deals and also the scene of frequent shootings, and Bob
and Randy said that we were almost certain to get shot there,
so that was out.

But in spite of those reasonable limitations, that still left
huge parts of the city, mostly south of Market Street, where
we would find countless homeless people. It was a big area,
and those still relatively dangerous regions kept us busy all
night. And admittedly now and then we strayed into places
we shouldn't have, where we'd promised not to go, but we
tried not to stay long and moved on as fast as was practical.
Bob and Randy advised us that wherever we went, the goal
was to get in and out fast, not to give people too much time to
think about it or attack us if we were in a tight situation in a
tough neighborhood. In the gentler places, we could stay longer, but they still urged us to move quickly. It's a policy we

stuck with and that always worked well for us, even when we made mistakes and wound up where we shouldn't. Moving at high speeds served us well every time. We didn't need to linger, we gave what we had and got out. We were there to get a job done, not hang out.

Another agreement we made early on was what to do if someone tried to hijack the van. Many people living on the streets have weapons. Some have guns, but knives were more current, and getting stabbed was a real possibility for us, working at close range. More than once I asked myself what I was doing. I am a single mother of eight children who need me. Risking getting killed on the streets wasn't sensible, yet I had an overwhelming need to continue what I'd started, as did the others. But I had a strong sense of responsibility to the rest of the team too. I worried a lot about them getting hurt, and we all kept a watchful eye and tried to cover each other's backs whenever we could. It wasn't always possible, but at least we tried. Despite that, we split up at times or found ourselves alone, surrounded by sometimes hostile homeless men. But we were both sensible and lucky, and I'm deeply grateful that none of us ever got hurt.

We agreed that if anyone ever attacked us for the vans or what was in them, we would give up the vehicles immediately. There was no point dying for a van full of sleeping bags. So we would hand over the keys with no argument, no questions asked. It never happened, fortunately, but at least we were all clear on our priorities and had a plan, if things went wrong.

We tried other safety measures over the years, none of which really worked. A few years into it, we decided to add two-way radios, since we so often split up and strayed from each other when we got busy. We tried to stay in pairs but often got spread out. There were always a few of us at the vans, handing things out, but most of the others wandered off to round people up, and make sure we found everyone we had gone there to find, in hidden doorways, in dark alleys, or under freeway ramps. Being able to communicate by radio in the event of danger or injury, or just to say how many people were in a camp around the corner, would have helped us out a lot and made us both safer and more efficient. The first time the people on the streets saw us with radios, they ran like mice: They thought we were all cops. I don't think we used the radios, in all, for more than an hour, if that. Bad idea. Forget that. What we eventually settled on as our only safety device were whistles, worn around our necks to use in case of emergency, which was a sensible idea. We never had to use them. The team, however, did use theirs at every opportunity— every time I reached into the doughnut box. It did not deter me, unfortunately. I managed to scarf down two or three doughnuts every time we went out. I ignored the whistles and

figured the doughnuts were worth it! And I got hungry jumping out of the van all night. So I endured the humiliation of
them whistling at me, and ate another doughnut.

A new element that the two police officers had added on
their first trip was the addition of a greeting, "Yo!" I don't
know if it's a cop thing, a guy thing, or a street thing, but their
form of greeting as we approached people was "Yo!" A very
loud "Yo!," in fact. One of our cautions was not to startle people. People on the streets are wary and sometimes frightened.
They live in danger, and mental illness is no stranger on the
streets. You don't want to tiptoe up on people discreetly and
scare them to death at close range, or wake them out of a
sound sleep by frightening them. Their reaction could have
been dangerous. So we gave lots of warning that we were ap-
proaching, so people had time to evaluate the situation and
feel comfortable with it—or, rarely, tell us not to, if they didn't
want us around. They had that right. It was their space, not
ours. And Bob and Randy's "Yo!" definitely did the job of
warning people when we approached. I have one of those
mouse voices that even when I think I'm shouting, people say
"What?" And when I'm talking normally, no one can hear me.
I am painfully shy in real life, and have a very soft voice. My
first "Yo!" was beyond pathetic. It was a baby whisper that
sounded like half of "yoyo," said by a six-year-old. It took me a

while to grow my "Yo" into something impressive. By now I have a "Yo," I am proud to say, that could knock you flat on your ass.

"Yo!" is a greeting familiar to people on the street, and they use it to catch your attention and stop you in your tracks.

We were getting back into the van on our first night out as a team, after one of our stops, when a man came running down the street as fast as he could, to stop us before we left. I saw him coming from the distance, desperate to get what we had to give. Into the night, in our direction, he shouted, "Yo! Angel!" We waited for him, and I was startled by what he'd said. He thanked us profusely for what we were doing, and said we must be angels coming to help others. We gave him what he needed, and off he went, leaving with us the gift of our name, as a group. We called our outreach team thereafter "Yo! Angel!"

Another extraordinary thing happened to us that night. We were cruising along slowly beneath an underpass, looking for people sleeping there, and there were a lot of them. Suddenly on a support post for the underpass, we saw a large chalk drawing. It stopped us all. It was a beautiful painting of a boy, done in pastel colors, and he had wings. There was our angel. A sign, after we had just been called that, deservedly or not. But what stopped me and mesmerized me, as tears sprang to my eyes, was that the boy in the lovely angel drawing looked just like my son Nick. He was the angel in our midst. John and Jane returned days later to take a photograph of it, which they had put on a sweatshirt for me, as a gift. I treasure it still. It was the perfect sign for our first night together as a team, the night Yo! Angel! was born.

We became Yo! Angel! that night, and so did the foundation I founded years later, to help us manage our finances and make the most of every dollar we spent on the streets. Jane saw to it that we had a sign that said "Protected by angels" hanging from the rearview mirror, and various little angel mascots. The occasionally outrageous jokes we told between stops did not qualify us as angels, but they kept our spirits up, and we all liked the idea of angels as our theme.

Although our distribution went fairly smoothly, it was nonetheless complicated fishing things out of the van, making sure everyone had one of each item: sleeping bag, jacket, gloves, hat, socks. We had added a wool beanie, which was useful on cold nights on the streets. I wore one myself. Sometimes people wanted two pairs of socks, or a jacket for an absent husband or girlfriend. We gave them what they wanted, but running the supplies out of the back of the van was like a discount store on the day of a half-price sale. We did a lot of business quickly, and Jane had to stay on her toes to keep the rest of us from turning our supplies into a junk heap for her to deal with. She was always a good sport about the mess we made as we handed things out at a fast pace, and people were patient as they waited for us to turn back to them with our arms full of things they needed. It was only the beginning for us, and we still had a lot to learn about what was needed and what worked.

In the spirit of that innocence and newness, we managed to drive headfirst into a one-way dead-end alley south of Market Street, where we saw two or three people asleep in doorways. It looked like an easy stop to us, and no big deal. But once we were deep into the alley, with another van behind us and no way out except to back up, about forty young men poured out from doorways and nooks and crannies where we hadn't seen them as we drove in. They were a rough crowd, and just about all of them looked high on drugs. The alley was closer than we should have been to the very dangerous Sixth Street, where we had agreed not to go. The alley had seemed okay. It wasn't, and we found ourselves instantly surrounded and outnumbered by a large group of very angry-looking young men, who began jostling each other and us, afraid that we wouldn't have enough for all of them. We were hugely outnumbered, three or four to one. They were pushing, shoving, and shouting, and in our nervousness, one of us accidentally locked the van with the keys in it, so we were stuck on the street with the men, locked out of our van. I took one look at the situation, and religious or not, I said the only thing one could in that situation, which didn't look good to any of us. I muttered, "Oh shit!" In all honesty, I figured we were going to be killed.

We had the other van to escape to, but we still had one locked van with the motor running that we couldn't get into. Five of us, panicked, scrambling into the unlocked van, was the kind of exit from the situation we'd all hoped to avoid. Within seconds, Randy gave one of his bellowing "Yo"s, told everyone to line up single file, and informed them loudly that we had more than enough to go around. Much to my amazement, they grumbled, but even in their bleary-eyed, aggressive state, they lined up single-file. Randy looked calm and in control. Our other men kept a watchful eye on the situation, and Jane and I sorted through jackets, hats, and the rest, and handed them out with lightning speed. Tony found a spare set of keys to our van in his, and we were able to unlock it.

We handed out everything we needed to, the men we were serving calmed down, and within a few minutes, the first van was backing out of the alley. Jane and I sailed into the back of our van through the back doors, and landed flat on our faces on a stack of sleeping bags, laughing nervously. A moment later, our doors were closed, and we were gone.

All's well that ends well, but it had been a more stressful situation than any of us liked, and we all agreed: No more dead ends, and next time we check it out more carefully before we just hop out. That didn't stop us from getting into a few narrow squeaks at other times, but little by little we learned the things we had to do to stay safe, and what to look out for. For our first night together as a larger team, it had gone pretty well, with only a few minor hiccups here and there, the dead-end alley being one of them. Jane and I still laugh at the way we sailed into the van that night. I swear we looked like we were flying, but the truth is, we were damn lucky to get out.

We gave away a hundred of everything that night. There were the now all-too-familiar touching, poignant moments, and the last stop that ripped your heart out. It never failed. We had left my house in good spirits, making jokes and munching doughnuts, but as we drove home, and as it would always be from then on, we rode in silence, thinking about the people we had seen, the moments we had shared, and embedding every one of them deep into our hearts. Everyone knew then, just as I had weeks before, that what we were seeing had already changed our lives. How could it not? We would have had to be dead not to absorb into our souls all that we were seeing every time we went out. We took a part of them home with us, and left part of ourselves with them on the streets.

FOUR

What Are We Doing to Help?
Or Not.

One thing I was shocked to learn once I began working on the streets was how hostile the city was to the homeless, while claiming otherwise. I suspect that may be true in almost all cities. I never see homeless in Beverly Hills, so where do they put them? What do they do to move them away or hide them? New York has its homeless, yet the city claims they have made vast inroads into the problem. Really? How? Informed sources say that one of New York's best tools to deal with the homeless is bus tickets to New Jersey. Likewise, at one time San Francisco had a program to give them bus tickets to anywhere but here. Just get them out! It's a modern-day version of the pea-under-the-shell game. Just move it around to somewhere else, and hide it there.

Civic leaders in every city find homeless people lingering

Danielle Steel

on the streets and in doorways an embarrassment. They want them to go away. Merchants complain that the homeless interfere with business. And there are programs in every city designed to assist them to get off the streets, or so they say. But in truth only the most functional among the homeless are able to access those programs. Lines are endless, forms are impossible to decipher, qualifications can't be met, standards don't apply. Waiting lists for every kind of facility keep people on hold for months for medical care, detox programs, housing. Some waits are as long as a year, while those on the lists grow despondent, get sicker and more desperate, or die. Funding is being slashed and eliminated at an alarming rate, so some programs disappear entirely while potential clients languish to no avail.

One of the methods of dealing with the homeless is called creaming, which is scooping the "cream" off the top and helping those who are most able. But those who are less capable, less functional, more disturbed or damaged, or mentally ill sink to the bottom of the system like rocks, where no one helps them. Those were the people we looked for when we did outreach on the streets: the ones who couldn't get to free dining rooms, and the many who were often justifiably afraid of shelters, or too disturbed to be allowed to enter them, and had no idea how to fill out forms to access help. They are the truly forgotten people of the streets, and the ones in greatest need. If we don't reach out to them, who will? Almost no one does.

I don't know about you, but going to the DMV gives me the vapors, standing in line at a department store makes me hysterical, and looking at a six-page form of any kind makes me feel brain dead. How is someone who is already in dire straits and often disoriented supposed to access help in a system where even trying to reach someone by phone puts you in cyberhell? Today calling a doctor, an insurance company, the post office, a passport agency, an airline, or even local information is a nightmare. How are people who are already in shaky shape supposed to deal with that? They don't. They just give up. And worse yet, the agencies and people who are supposed to help them are overworked and understaffed and give up too.

There are far too few real, accessible programs for the homeless in every city. Philadelphia is said to be the best in the country in dealing with homelessness. I have no firsthand experience with that city. In San Francisco, where everyone on the streets readily agrees that the shelters are extremely dangerous, in order to get in, you have to be there by six o'clock, and one of the criteria for entry is that you not exhibit "bizarre behavior." By definition, living on the streets can be called bizarre behavior. How many of us would qualify as *not* having bizarre behavior? And not everyone who wants to be in a shelter can get there precisely by six, or earlier if they need to line up. How easy are we making life for these people? Or more precisely, how difficult? And how realistic are we? Do we really have to make their lives so much more difficult than they already are?

The system I saw used most frequently to address the homeless was harassment. When I first began working on the streets, I kept hearing about the dreaded DPW. I had no idea what that was. The KGB maybe, with new initials? What exactly was this agency so feared among the homeless? I was soon to learn that it is the Department of Public Works. The theory is that if people are going to "insist" on living on the streets, then the city will just have to clean them up, tidy them up, and teach them a thing or two. Admittedly, the belongings of homeless people look messy. But how neat can you be when you're living in a cardboard box, and everything you own is in a shopping cart with three wheels? The DPW solves that problem. They arrive with a giant dump truck, and if the homeless person is momentarily away at a public bathroom, trying to scrounge up something to eat, trying to find work, or maybe just asleep, the DPW truck scoops up all their belongings, and tidies up the mess for them. And suddenly the homeless person has no bedding, no clothes, and so little to their name that you weep to see it. After the DPW truck does its job, they have absolutely nothing at all except the shirts on their backs, and rubber flip-flops they found in a trashcan somewhere. The DPW goes out there to break up "camps," scoop up "cribs," and get rid of all the unsightly "debris" that is all the homeless person has in the world.

One of the theories is that if a homeless person has nothing to survive with, you can force them off the streets. It doesn't work like that. There is nowhere else for them to go. Some are too physically and mentally sick to do anything other than what they're doing, and rather than helping, or getting them into a safe place, or nurturing them in some way, the DPW takes away what little they do have and leaves them even more helpless and ill-equipped to survive than before. I'm sorry, but to me that's harassment. We have to do a whole lot better than just hauling away their belongings in a garbage truck, leaving them crying on the street. I have rarely seen anything more heartless than that single tactic, which leaves people even more deprived and even more destroyed, and teaches them despair as a way of life. Just how cruel does a city have to be?

Several years ago, while they were building the new baseball stadium in San Francisco, there was an area of undeveloped land nearby where homeless people set up a camp. At one time, it must have housed close to two hundred people in tents, cardboard boxes, sleeping bags, and small makeshift constructions. There are advantages to camps like that, in that they afford some form of protection to more vulnerable members of the group. There is usually safety in numbers, though not always. I watched that camp set up and grow over many months. It was a small city unto itself, and ran in an orderly fashion. And then one day we came along with our vans, and what we saw looked like a hurricane had hit it.

Nothing was left but small bits of debris that had been rolled over and crushed beneath the wheels of giant trucks. DPW trucks had demolished the camp earlier that day, scooping up everyone's belongings and flattening what was left. By the time we got there, dozens of quietly sobbing people were standing around in shock, with nothing left. It was the kind of scene you see after an earthquake hits a village. There had been no time to salvage what they needed or what was important to them. The camp was flattened, destroyed, disposed of, and everything they owned with it.

How can any city talk about how it is addressing "the homeless problem" while treating human beings in this appalling, dehumanizing way? I can't begin to tell you how often we stopped our vans and found devastated people, crying that the DPW had just taken everything they owned. My stomach turned over every time I heard it. I've looked into their faces and seen their eyes, the tears rolling down their cheeks. If that's the best we can do to solve the problem, it's a sorry statement about us and our cities. And sadly, I see just as many people on the streets as I did fourteen years ago, if not more. In fact, I am certain that there are more homeless people on the streets each year, particularly in these troubled economic times.

San Francisco has for years used an absurdly haphazard system to provide a head count of the homeless. Once a year, a handful of people go out on foot in a prescribed area where the homeless are presumed to live. The census counters walk the streets for that one night a year and count them. As the director of one of the agencies providing free mental health services says, the Audubon Society spends more time, care, and money counting birds than we do counting homeless people.

During that one night of "homeless counting," they count whoever they see. Anyone in a shelter, in a bathroom, buying coffee at McDonald's, eating in a free dining room, or lucky enough to be in a hotel room for one night is overlooked, not included in the count. As a result, the officially listed numbers have nothing to do with reality, with the true number of people on the streets. A few years ago, the number of homeless people in San Francisco was listed as just over 7,000. At one time, the official count had dropped to just over 5,000. (Was it a cold night when they counted? Were most people off the streets, or hiding? Had their disability checks just arrived, so many escaped to hotels for a single night? Or did fewer people do the count?)

The church that provides the most homeless services in the city, and serves over one million free meals a year, believes the more accurate homeless count on San Francisco's streets at that time was closer to 20,000. The police who worked on the streets in the areas where most homeless people live agreed that there were more than 20,000 people living on the streets. My uneducated rough guess, just based on the population we served (about 3,000 people a year), was also 20,000. That's a far cry from the official count of 5,000 to 7,000, which misleads citizens into believing that the problem is less severe than it is.

Misrepresenting the count lulls us into a false sense of security that the problem is being solved. The reality is very different. The growing population of homeless in all our cities is a strong indicator that whatever help we're offering is missing its mark. However good our intentions, however many programs we have in place, the people in most dire need of them are getting lost, not benefiting from the system, and not getting the help they need. And without help they will not be able to get off the streets.

We need more programs, more money, more help, more workers, more people who care about the problem of homelessness, more citizens who are willing to see it and do whatever they can to help. Until then, ignoring the problem entirely, or harassing the homeless, is not the answer or the solution. The solution is greater awareness, more available funding, and more help.

One of the things that struck me once I began working on the streets was the variety of people I met there. Strangely, each trip was different, in the age and race of people we saw, and I was never quite sure why. Sometimes I saw mostly older (maybe forties and fifties) African American men, up to 75 percent on some nights. Other times we saw mostly Caucasians, the majority in their thirties, who looked functional, freshly on the streets, and as though they could be part of the normal workforce, although something had clearly gone wrong in their lives. Women were always in the minority, and if only recently arrived on the streets they sometimes seemed in better shape than the men. Newly arrived women appeared less unkempt. Sometimes we saw women who'd been there longer and were absolutely ravaged. I had the feeling that women don't hold up long term. (Our ratio was usually ten men to one woman on any given night, except sometimes in warmer weather when there were a few more women out there. In cold winter weather, the women were more likely to go inside, despite the violence in the shelters, except the most hardcore who were too far gone to even get to shelter, so we went to them.) A woman I had seen frequently died last year. I assumed she was somewhere in her sixties. I was shocked when I read her obituary to discover that she had once been a model, and was thirty-two or -three when she died.

One of the most moving examples I've seen was a young woman who must have been in her twenties. She was wearing a flowered silk dress on a summer night, her hair was combed, and she was wearing a string of fake pearls around her neck. She was one of the few people I continued to see regularly for eleven years. At first, I watched her deteriorate over the months, to a heartbreaking degree. The silk dress and pearls disappeared quickly. And ten years later, probably in her early thirties, she had lost all her teeth, had lost a leg, was in a wheelchair, wound up in jail from time to time, and had a look of devastation about her. Yet when I saw her—and I looked for her often—she was always courteous, kind, and smiling. We always stopped and chatted for a while, and she told me how things were going for her. We gave her our supplies, and she thanked us profusely every time. Clearly, the available systems weren't working for her. She lived in a tent on a street corner for years. I think drugs were probably involved, and maybe mental illness, or maybe not. All I saw was what happened to her since she'd been on the streets. I asked her no embarrassing questions. Her descent into hell, and how she got there, were none of my business. All I could do was visit her there every few weeks. I worried when I didn't see her. And what I worried about most was where would she go from here? Who would help her? How could she break the downward spiral? And why had no one helped her to get off the streets?

I don't know what gets people to the streets. Some people live so close to the edge that when enough things go wrong, they fall into the abyss of homelessness. Others are there only temporarily and can easily be helped or salvaged. Some have been there for so long that, like someone with a terminal illness, you know they will never be able to return to what they once were. Some struggle on, others have clearly given up. Some you can easily imagine filtering back into the mainstream, given half a chance, but others never fit, never have, and never will.

Far too many (the majority) appear to be suffering from some form of mental illness, and there is nowhere for them to go for assistance. Unable to access help on their own, abandoned by their families, or even with families who would want to help them but are unable to due to our legal system surrounding mental illness, these people get lost along the way. All of them are on the streets, and we are failing each one of them in some way.

Some people say that homelessness is a result of not having enough mental hospitals. But the problem is more complex.

Danielle Steel

Even if we had enough hospitals, we have no way of getting people into them and convincing them to stay there for treatment. It is an unpopular opinion with most people except the most experienced professionals, but I have long felt that our current system, where mentally ill people must agree to be hospitalized unless they have proven themselves to be a danger to society is a nice theory, but just doesn't work. Right now, in our current system, the decision to be hospitalized rests in the mentally ill person's hands. It's up to them. And realistically, many or even most of them are not in a position to make that decision for themselves. Families with mentally ill relatives can do nothing to get them off the streets, or hospitalize them for treatment. I am deeply grateful that I never got to that place with my son Nick. As many of us do, I have several friends who have adult children (some in their thirties and forties) who have been homeless and lost to them for years. There is absolutely nothing the parents can do about it, and sometimes they wind up in jail rather than hospitals if they step over the line society sets for them, or exhibit behavior that breaks a law.

I believe we need laws that allow us to hospitalize people when necessary, for treatment and safekeeping, even without their consent. Perhaps the people who make the laws, or the citizens who vote for them, have no idea how vulnerable the mentally ill are on the streets, and what very real danger they are in. The laws we have now are well-intentioned, and do avoid the situations we all read about years ago, when some unsuspecting mentally healthy person could be put away in a mental hospital against their will, often as a result of their family's greed or self-serving motives. Today's laws prevent that from happening, but the net is so broad now that we can no longer hospitalize those who need it most. Our hands are tied. So instead of getting treatment, or being helped by those who care about them, mentally ill people are homeless on the streets. The general consensus is that 80 to 90 percent of homeless people are suffering from some form of mental illness, and they're not getting the help they need.

In San Francisco, a statute of the health code called a 5150 allows you to hospitalize persons exhibiting inappropriate or bizarre behavior for seventy-two hours for evaluation. That gives mental health professionals three days to study their behavior and make a decision as to whether or not they are a danger to themselves or others. If not, it is nearly impossible to extend the three days for a longer period (with the help of a 5250). But sometimes it takes longer than three days to assess a psychiatric problem. And it seems to me that it's not enough time to determine if they are indeed a danger to themselves or others. And what if others are a danger to them? We can't hospitalize these people to protect them, no matter how vulnerable their state or confused their mind. As long as they are not "dangerous," they are free to go, back to a world where they are preyed upon, in constant danger, and in no condition to cope with the rigors of street life or the constant threats lurking there. Sometimes, no matter how sad, that decision should be taken out of their hands.

Homelessness is not just about not having a job or an apartment. Too often homelessness is due to a disordered mind. It's more obvious in some cases than others, and some people are less able to comply with society's rules than others. But in far too many cases, the mentally ill are falling through the cracks and have nowhere to go. You see them pushing their carts as they talk to themselves, sleeping in doorways, living in cardboard boxes, soaking wet and freezing cold. They are no danger to you, perhaps, but they are unable to help themselves. And those of us who so desperately want to take care of them, family or others, have no way to reach out to them, get help, or bring them home. I think it is one of society's greatest problems today, an urban problem that is out of control, and our existing laws are doing nothing to help us stem the tide.

In this instance, laws that protect a few are hurting many, many more. It hurts to put someone in a mental hospital. I know. I've done it. But it hurts far, far more to see them flounder on the street, and perhaps watch them die there when they wouldn't otherwise. Simply put, we need better, more efficient laws to help solve the problem. And the reality is that even many who seem functional at first glance really aren't.

I believe only a tiny fraction of people are on the streets because of slim savings, mismanaged funds, or the loss of a job. Most of the homeless are there because they cannot function in our society, and are too disabled in some way to access the help they need. They are lost out there on their own. It's up to us to find them and do something to help. Like drowning people, they can't save themselves. If they are to be saved, it's up to us, the functioning members of society, to do it. If they were capable of doing it, they wouldn't be out there. So what do we do now? Turn our backs and let them drown, or do something about it? I hope that our communal answer will be to reach out a hand and help in any way we can, large or small. And in time, our legislators need to address the issues by providing better laws to allow us to help them.

Homelessness is not one of the "sexy" or appealing causes that make people rush forward to help. For the most part, the homeless are not adorable, appealing children with sunny smiles. They are tired and broken, they have lost teeth and arms and legs from festering wounds. They smell bad, they need a bath. They frighten us, not just in their appearance or behavior, but because if we look at them more closely, we cannot help but fear that something similar could happen to us or someone we love. But just as much as any of our friends or relatives, they desperately need our help. Like most children, they cannot find their way back by themselves. We *have* to help.

FIVE

The Clients:
Who Are They?

Although it's not unusual for me to forget the name or face of someone I meet at a dinner party, I rarely forgot a face I saw on the street. Some of them I saw time and time again, others I saw once and then they disappeared forever. I always wondered what happened to them. Did they move on to another city? Did they go to a shelter? Had family members claimed them and convinced them to come home? Did they go to jail? Or did they die? I heard of deaths on the streets often. Whatever happened to them, there are faces I will remember forever, even though I will never know their stories. I never, ever asked them how they got to the streets. I felt I owed them that respect. And street etiquette and simple decency forbade it.

The woman I saw most often is the one I mentioned earlier,

who began her life on the streets in a blue flowered silk dress and a string of pearls and ended up in a wheelchair, missing all her teeth and one leg. Yet she was always cheerful, polite, kind, and grateful for our kindness and anything we gave her. She was a bright woman, and I know she had children somewhere. She mentioned them, and as in the case of many women on the streets, her children were with her mother. (In other cases women on the streets have children in foster care.)

One of the people I met on one of my first trips was a man who popped out of a Dumpster, like a genie out of a bottle. At another time and place, he would have scared the life out of me, and I have to admit, even that night he frightened me a little. His hair was a tangle of dreads and his face was streaked with dirt, he was filthy, and his eyes were wild. Trying to maintain my composure, I explained to him what I had to offer him, and he nodded, standing in the Dumpster. I ran to the van to get him a sleeping bag and jacket, after he told me what size he was. With them, I handed him a hat, socks, and gloves. All of it disappeared into the bowels of the Dumpster where he was living. And being very small, I couldn't see into it. I was just walking away, when I heard his voice shout out behind me: "How do I look?" I turned to see him beaming at me, in the same extreme state of disarray, but he had added to it the clean, warm jacket. I think on that trip the jackets we gave out were pale gray. (We always took whatever colors we could get in volume. For obvious reasons, we preferred darker colors, but couldn't always get them.) As I turned to look at him, I had never seen a smile so wide and proud. He was absolutely exploding with joy. The tenderness of the moment brought tears to my eyes, as I smiled back at him. Along with a warm jacket, we had somehow given him back humanity and pride.

"You look beautiful!" I shouted back at him and meant it, and his smile widened.

"Thank you!" he said. No one had touched my heart as he did at that moment. I still think of him often, and privately call him "How do I look?" to identify him when we talk about him. He looked so happy, and it was an infinitely precious moment. As I waved again and walked back to the van, he shouted "God bless you!" and vanished into the Dumpster. I never saw him again, but like so many others, I will remember him always.

Another woman I saw only once was pushing a shopping cart at midnight, near San Francisco's civic center. At one time, there was a tent city there, which was disbanded by the DPW. Afterward, people camped in doorways and on steps, in clusters of cardboard boxes, especially for the night. She was a large woman, pushing her cart with a measured step and a dignified walk, and for some crazy reason, she reminded me of English nannies I had seen pushing prams around the park in my childhood. Everything she owned was in that cart, stacked high but in meticulous order. It was one of our last trips before Christmas. We approached her, told her what we had. As we spoke, I noticed that she had done her hair in little ponytails and knots all over her head. And from each tiny tail and knot she had hung a silver Christmas ball. She was a bit like a human Christmas tree, or one of those holiday cards showing a reindeer with Christmas balls hanging from its antlers. It sounds crazy, but I loved it. Holidays are seldom acknowledged on the street. And my heart ached each time I said, "Happy Thanksgiving" or "Merry Christmas." Just saying it seemed like an affront to people so intent on the business of living and survival. *Happy? Merry?* Ugh. How insulting is that, in the circumstances they're in? Sometimes I just couldn't bring myself to say it. But the woman with a head full of silver Christmas balls had clearly decided to pay homage to the season.

As we handed her the things we were giving her, she looked me in the eye with a serious sense of purpose. She didn't smile as she glanced at me intently. "My name is Brenda," she said clearly. "Please don't forget me." "I won't," I promised, wondering how many people had forgotten her, wherever she came from. "I promise," I said out loud. And I never have. Each time I drive by there, I think of Brenda with her proud walk and noble stance, with the silver ornaments in her hair. I will never forget Brenda. How could I?

Similarly, we found many of our clients outside the bus station, lined up in the shelter of an overhang, safer than most because of bright lights that allowed no one to sneak up on them. It was a place where we did a lot of business. It rapidly became one of our regular stops. And one night, in the midst of the controlled chaos of handing bags with contents in three sizes out of three vans, a man walked up to me quietly, looked at me intently, and said, "My name is Jerry. Will you pray for me?" I thought he meant right then, and I would have if he wanted. We had never done that before, but no one had ever asked. "Now?" I asked quietly, honored that he should ask. "No." He shook his head, his eyes never leaving mine, "Later . . . after you go . . . pray for Jerry." I have now for years. His name is carved into my mind. The promise was real.

A woman who tore my heart out crossed our path in our first year. She was young and blond and pretty, maybe in her early twenties. It was the first time I learned what a crib was. In her case, it was a well-constructed shelter made of boxes carefully fit together, propped between two pillars of an overpass. She emerged from her boxes, shivering in the cold, and I correctly guessed her to be six months pregnant. I was deeply concerned for her and we talked about her pregnancy. She said she was getting prenatal care from time to time, though not on a regular basis. And what we had to give her seemed so inadequate, living on the streets in her condition. She said she was living alone, then added that this was her third baby. She said that when she gave birth, the social services took the babies, and then she returned to the streets. She said it with tears in her eyes, but a plucky tilt to her chin. I didn't dare ask her where her family was, if they would help her, or how all this had happened. But she kept my stomach churning after I left her that night. How could she go through all that and then give up her baby? But what would happen to an infant on the streets, living as she did? It made me think of women in war zones, whom you see on TV, or in ravaged countries. And here this was, happening in our backyard, in an allegedly civilized city. Later I learned of one government agency and a group of private volunteers who provide prenatal care to the homeless, and I have referred many women to them. But I did not know of them then.

We saw her regularly over the next months, as she got closer to having the baby. It was spring by then. She never complained, she was just grateful for what we gave her. She would take what we offered and disappear into her little cardboard box. She had no one with her, no one to help her. And then one day, when we came back to find her, her crib was gone—"crib" being an appropriate word in her case. The cardboard was folded and lying on the street. I could only assume that the baby had come, and I had no idea where she was. I never saw her again, and have no notion of where she is now. The saddest thing, in all of these cases, particularly with older people you see on the streets, is that when they vanish, you have no idea if their condition is better or worse. You have no idea if they've gone inside, moved away, are sick somewhere, or have died. All of these people who have carved their faces into my heart and memory may no longer be alive. And yet they live on in my head. Brenda, Jerry ... "How do I look?" ... the young pregnant mother ... the girl in the wheelchair with one leg who once wore pearls ... They are embedded in my soul and my memories.

Another man who made a deep impression lined up behind our vans when we pulled up at the public library. We had to be careful in that location, because sometimes there were large numbers of people, as many as forty or fifty. It was also a short distance from Market Street, where we knew drug deals went down. Once people heard that we'd arrived, once they knew about us, they'd flock to us in droves. And if we ran out of supplies, we could be in real danger and deep trouble. Aside from that, I hated disappointing anyone out there; that's not why we were there. But we also had to consider the risks. And running out of supplies among desperate people, particularly if there were drugs involved, could have been very dangerous for us. So we were careful where we stopped, and how many people were around, and that we had enough supplies on hand.

But on that particular night, it seemed quiet at the library. There were about thirty people lined up behind the van. There was a homeless young skateboarder doing flips and tricks on the library steps, and he came back and forth to chat with us, as others stood waiting peacefully. It was all men that night. And I noticed a man far back in the line, in a business suit, white shirt, and tie, and immediately frowned disapproval. I was afraid he was just there to get something free, and he wasn't homeless. I said something to one of my co-workers, asking what he was doing in the line, and my colleague said that he was okay, he had seen him come out of a sleeping bag on the library steps.

Every now and then, as we worked in less ravaged neighborhoods, people would approach with curiosity. When they saw what we were doing, they sometimes said something kind to us. And only a handful over all those years tried to take advantage of an opportunity for something free, although they weren't homeless. I suspected the man in the suit of that. The information that he'd been sleeping on the library steps reassured me, but we had never come across anyone like him on the streets. Some of the people we dealt with were still surprisingly clean, like a few young men who were homeless but trying to get jobs, who kept their hair combed and their faces well shaven, and wore clean running shoes for a while (they get dirty quickly). But no one had ever shown up in a suit and tie. I was more than startled.

I hung around the back of the van to get a better look at him as he approached, and finally he was next in line for our supplies. He met my eyes, and I smiled at him. No way was I going to say "What are *you* doing here?" but he volunteered his own story, which was extremely rare on the streets. What shocked me most was not only was he wearing a good-looking dark-gray striped business suit, a clean white shirt, and a sober tie he had loosened, but his shoes were polished. He wore rimless glasses and had a good haircut. I guessed him to be in his late fifties. He looked like my banker, anyone's stockbroker, or some of my friends. I would never in a hundred million years have guessed that he was homeless. If you had introduced me to him and said that to me, I wouldn't have believed you. How could this be?

He never gave his name, although some people do as though to make a mark of some kind and be remembered. He said that he had been an executive in Silicon Valley and his wife had left him not long before. They were vastly overextended and heavily in debt, he had lost everything and then lost his job. He was trying to find employment in his field, and no one knew he was homeless, not even his family. He hung around and talked to us for a while, hungry for conversation.

For whatever reason, he had decided not to go to a shelter—scared maybe, with good reason. Shelters are dangerous enough for people who don't look like him. And he would have stuck out like a sore thumb and been an instant target. Eventually, we had to go, and we watched him walk slowly up the library steps with what we'd given him. He had been extremely grateful, and before he left us, we wished him good luck finding a job. But he had shaken us all. With many of the homeless people we saw, it was hard to find the bridge between us other than our common humanity. We could no longer see where they came from, and we met them only with compassion. But this man had the kind of story that strikes fear in people's hearts. A series of mistakes, some bad luck, too much spending, a broken marriage, a lost job at the wrong time. It happens to many, although they are the most likely to get off the streets again, as long as drugs and alcohol aren't involved. Thinking about him, we were all silent on the way home. He was God's Last-Stop Curve Ball that night.

Another pair I always remember with a smile were most likely teenagers, somewhere between sixteen and eighteen, although they looked fairly adult. It was very rare for us to see adolescents, and never children. Homeless children are almost instantly picked up by the police and taken to shelters, hopefully with their parents. In eleven years I never saw a child on the streets—many pregnant bellies, but never an infant or a child. Ever. And I'd say teenagers (in groups of two or three, and rarely but occasionally a camp of as many as eight or ten) were five to every six hundred adults. They tended not to hang out in the same places as adults, and kept to themselves. In San Francisco, they were mostly in an area called the Panhandle, which was too dangerous for us, climbing through shrubbery and bushes in the dark.

Also, many kids on the streets had the reputation for doing drugs. They were more likely to sell what we gave them than adults. We saw our clients put their new clothes on immediately and we knew they didn't sell them. There were plenty of drugs among the adults, but rarely did they sell the supplies we handed out. Their need was too great, their gratitude evident as we watched them dive into the bags and put on the jackets immediately. And as I drove around the city between trips, leading my own life, I so often saw the familiar black bags that we used to hold the supplies we gave perched atop shopping carts, their prized possession—so I knew these bags were not being sold.

Kids on the streets are a whole different breed. And when I say "kids," I mean adolescents. Most of them, I fear, are out there because they have lived with such shocking abuses at home that whatever evils they meet in the streets couldn't possibly be worse than what happened to them at home. Some are on drugs. Some have been out there for years. It's not unusual to talk to a seventeen-year-old who will tell you that he or she has been out there for four or five years. They have no desire to go home, and will grow up on the streets, doing what they can to survive. Many have come from other places and cities; some want to go back home but can't afford to or organize it. They tend to stay in groups. I have never seen an adolescent alone or even with adults. They almost always tell you that they are older than they are. Almost all believe that they will "get it together" one day, and many can, with the right help from the right hands. They have a sturdy, determined look about them. Life is still ahead of them, and despite whatever hardships they've encountered, many will survive.

They were the hardest for me to walk away from when we left, because they reminded me so much of my children, and I wished we could do more for them, although they were often leery of us. They didn't want to be taken anywhere, sent home, or dragged off the streets against their will. The one thing I always did was call a remarkable San Francisco organization called Larkin Street Youth Services, which is set up to assist young people with medical care, shelter, education, finding jobs, drug treatment or rehab, a program for kids with AIDS, or reunification with their families if desirable. Their street teams reach out both with vehicles and on foot, and I always let them know the location of young people I saw, knowing they would go out to them. I hoped the street teams could talk them into going inside. Sometimes they succeeded and some-times they didn't, but they always tried.

So running into adolescents was rare for us. On one par-ticular night we were in a back alley, and I can't remember if it was a tent or pile of cardboard boxes we spotted, but out of it emerged a couple of teenagers about sixteen or eighteen right out of a movie or off a CD cover or on MTV. I had never seen such dazzling punk gear in my life: spikes and chains, leather and red plaid. The girl was wearing a pair of knee-high com-bat boots. He had a towering mohawk that was glued into place. They had piercings and tattoos on every surface, but in their own crazy way, they were so beautiful to look at, and so extreme, that all of us smiled. We chatted with them for a while, gave them our stuff, and didn't intrude on them fur-ther. They wanted no additional help. And in their own outra-geous way, they were one of the prettiest sights of the night. They weren't God's Last-Stop Curve Ball—we came upon them halfway through the night and they boosted our spirits for a long time.

There are a thousand other such stories, all of them gut-wrenching, touching, funny, devastating, heartbreaking, like the woman who leapt up from her rags and boxes in a door-way and said, "How did you know? It's my birthday!" She was ecstatic, and we all hugged her and wished her a happy birth-day. One man was totally encased in a roll of tin foil he had found, to keep warm. We saw a woman with a dozen cats who we saw for close to a year, all of them on leashes. I was always afraid of the dogs out there. The people I met made their way into my heart within minutes, but their pit bulls and hungry mongrels never did. We had enough to think about, without worrying about getting attacked by dogs. I like dogs and have several of my own, but the dogs we saw on the streets scared me. The team often laughed at me for it. Show me a guy who looks like he might kill you, and most of the time, I could stand my ground. But show me a dog who bares his fangs at me, and I would run like hell, and babysit the dough-nuts till the rest of the team got back. Yeah, okay, and I ate a couple of the chocolate ones with sprinkles while I waited. No one's perfect.

SIX

Some Scary Moments

Not everyone we met on the street was friendly, though
we were remarkably lucky and had very few incidents.
On the whole, people met us with kindness and gratitude,
and sometimes concern for us. And then there were a few
who reminded us to keep our guard up, and be alert and
watchful. We were venturing into someone else's world, and a
hard one. We could have easily become targets for someone's
anger or frustration or fear. There were areas we stayed out of
by unanimous consent, as I've mentioned. We also decided,
after a few unnerving experiences, to avoid places where people were living in cars, old trucks, or school buses. The danger
for us there was that we couldn't see who was inside, how
many, or what was coming at us when the doors opened and
they came out. I liked working outdoors, seeing a wide area
where I was working, and who was around me, and who was

running toward us. I don't like surprises, and those buses and trucks were an invitation to bad surprises. After a few of those, we decided to avoid them. On the whole, we were pretty brave about the areas we ventured into. Some of what we did was just plain foolish, done in innocence and determination. But we were clearly blessed, and most of our clients were incredibly wonderful people. And sometimes even the less wonderful ones provided a certain kind of blessing.

We often reminded each other to look out for weapons as best we could. I suspect that many of the people we dealt with carried them, anything from handguns to knives and even razors. I have seen razors flashed next to a pant leg, then quietly slipped into a pocket. We were aware. But we also posed no threat. We wanted nothing from them—we gave, we didn't take. But in the case of someone mentally unstable, particularly if you startle, frighten, or worry them unduly, you can easily set them off. We gave plenty of warning as we approached, with that resounding "Yo!" We stayed plainly visible, we announced what we had to offer, and theoretically there was safety in numbers. There were almost always eleven of us in three vans, although admittedly once out of the vans, we spread out. We didn't mean to, and we tried to stay in pairs or groups, but sometimes there were too many people, spread out themselves, who needed us, or we drove into someplace darker than we expected, or there were thirty people hidden in the darkness when we thought there were only two or three. We took our chances on the streets like everyone else, no matter how careful we were.

The composition of the permanent team of Yo! Angel! was racially varied, so people were likely to be comfortable with some of us and not others. But there was a face and style for everyone. We were one North African, two Asian (one Japanese, one Chinese)—although you almost never see Asians homeless on the streets—two Hispanics, and six Caucasians. Of the eleven who composed the permanent team, three were women, eight were men. So there was pretty much a flavor, nationality, style, and gender for everyone's preferences about who to deal with. And we worked wonderfully as a team, and loved each other. The work we shared for so long was a powerful bond between us. We considered our street work a sacred engagement. Most of us just about never missed it, except in an emergency. My guess is that in eleven years, we each missed it once, twice at the most, and only for injury or illness. I stayed home once for a bad back, and worked on the streets with a cast on my leg for six months, with a torn Achilles tendon. None of us ever wanted to miss those nights, for whatever reason. We tried to get out to the streets about once a month from September through May.

The scary moments were overwhelmingly outweighed by the wonderful ones, for all of us. We acknowledged the hard incidents, and learned from them. In our very early days, we walked into a situation that looked like a fairly large and mixed group, and within minutes we realized that we had wandered into a group of homeless people being robbed by a bunch of young predators. It was a lesson for us, that the weakest and most unfortunate are preyed on by others who take what little they have. There is definitely a pecking order on the streets. We walked into the midst of that group like innocents, smiling happily at those we were about to help, as one of the predators looked at me and rolled his eyes. I was dressed in rough clothes, looking plain but clean, but probably even in my roughest gear, work boots and an old parka and wool cap, I looked pretty civilized. The leader of the predatorial group glanced at me in disbelief. "What are *you* doing here?" he asked with a wry grin, as we all realized the mistake we'd made. Trying to stop what was happening would have been too dangerous for us. We couldn't and we didn't, although I was sad about it. I explained rather nervously that we had brought some things to give away. He asked if there was enough for them, and we nodded. "Okay, leave some for us too, and go," he ordered. He was laughing by then, and even their victims were smiling a little. We must have looked pretty silly, Goody Two Shoes and Her Band of Merry Men walking right smack into the middle of something where we didn't belong and that was potentially very dangerous for us.

We left enough for everyone and got out quickly. We felt bad about the homeless people being ripped off, but we were extremely grateful that we hadn't been attacked. It was an early lesson in awareness on the streets. In some areas, even angels have to watch their backs. And it was a good warning to us to be more careful in the future. We constantly reminded each other to stay alert. It was easy to get too comfortable and cocky. That's usually when bad things happen.

Another time, I managed to get myself trapped at the back of the van, while waiting for clients. The person standing on the street, handing things out at the back of the van, ran the risk of being shoved up against it and getting squashed, if the recipients got too anxious or were too numerous. It was best not to be back there alone. I think Jane was standing near me, but everyone else had fanned out to find people as much as a block away. We were handing out stuff as fast as we could. I noticed, farther back in the line pressing against us, a man with intent, piercing eyes. He looked angry and nervous, and hostility oozed from him as I noticed his hand go to his waist-band and adjust something. It could have been a gun, but whatever it was, he was suddenly right up against me, looking down at me with an expression of suspicion and fury. "Why are you doing this?" he asked, referring to the things we were handing out. "Because I want to," I said as calmly as I could. "I think it's important and people need what we have to give." He stared at me for what seemed like an eternity, his eyes boring into mine, as I thought, *Shit, this guy is going to kill me.* We were belly to belly with a crowd pressing up behind him. I didn't move. I didn't want to make him angrier than he was, and then suddenly his hand left his waistband. He nodded, took what I'd been handing him, and glanced at me one last time as he murmured, "God bless you, Sister."

My knees were shaking when he left, and it was one of those times when I wondered if I was crazy to be out there, and asked myself what I was doing. Was our outreach work insanity or blessing? Sometimes it's hard to tell the difference. But I do know that I was braver on the streets than I have ever been anywhere—within reason, and with good friends close at hand. I wouldn't have done it alone, and couldn't have anyway, not on the scale we did. Although I'll admit, on very cold or rainy nights, I sometimes went out alone with supplies to give away. I couldn't stand lying in my comfy bed, thinking about them and not doing something about it.

On another night, we were handing things out on Market

Street. We had stopped to help a few homeless people in a doorway, and somehow in the wide expanse of open space on that street, people saw us, understood what we were doing, and came running. We were literally mobbed. Too many wanted too much and came at us too quickly. We had agreed on a signal if there was trouble. No questions asked, move fast, all we had to say was "Go! Go! Go!!" and talk about it later. Someone said it, Randy, I think, and we jumped into the vans, slammed the doors, and drove off, with people running after us. If they had been able to yank the doors open, they would have. But Younes, Paul, and either Bob or Tony were too fast for them. We took off like bats out of hell, and stayed off Market Street after that. It was too wide open, and we were too visible. The danger there was too great for us. We stuck to smaller, darker streets, where the challenges we were likely to meet were easier to control.

Probably one of the scariest nights, although nothing happened to us directly, made us realize how much danger we could be in. We ventured way too close to the infamous Sixth Street. Randy had warned us over and over we'd get hurt for sure if we went there, so we never did. But we were admittedly in the midst of the action that night, and felt uneasy. We saw some homeless people in doorways as we drove by so we made some quick drop-offs and took off.

Minutes later, police cars were whizzing by us. A lot of them. Helping the homeless is not illegal, but it is frowned on by local government, and at first we thought the police might be after us. We had researched the legalities of what we were doing before we even started. I knew for certain we were breaking no laws, absolutely none. But all city agencies, including the police, took a dim view of anyone helping the homeless. We were committing more of an unspoken city taboo than breaking any law, but we knew we'd get hassled if we got caught. I even wondered if they might throw me in jail, just to scare me. And I had long since volunteered to be the one to go, if that happened. After all, it was my fault we were doing it, so I was willing to go to jail, if need be. The four of our crew who were off-duty cops weren't breaking any laws or police rules either, but it was an unusual thing for them to do, so it might win them some heat. So for all those reasons, we had always avoided the police when we saw them. And that night, they were whizzing past us in droves.

A few phone calls to the right people informed us that someone had just been killed, literally a few feet from where we'd been working. The police were looking for the killer, still thought to be in the area. Another big wake-up call for us. People die on the streets, not just from starvation, exposure, infected wounds, or diseases. They also die from gunshot wounds and stabbings. It was sobering to think about. We finished handing out our supplies a few blocks away, and went home like chastised children. *A little more careful, please!* We got the message, and were grateful that our instincts had led us to move on.

SEVEN

Supplies . . . and Teddy Bears

A s things do in a conscientiously run operation, whatever
its kind, we evolved, and the nature and number of supplies we gave out altered over time. It took us, or me, a while
to figure out what our mission really was, beyond the original
message to "help the homeless." The question was, how? And
what was our goal? We weren't in a position to change their
situation, to get them off the streets permanently, house
them, detox them when necessary, or train them for jobs. We
couldn't solve the broader problem of homelessness, even
with eleven loving hearts and four vanloads of supplies. Our
nights on the street were both magical and grueling. And our
mission to keep homeless people alive for as long as possible,
until someone more skilled could help them in concrete ways,
worked well for them and for us, for a long time.

At one point, a friend of mine started a small bicoastal

program to job-train the most eligible homeless. It was a worthy cause, but for me it was still "creaming." He was scooping the best of the best off the top, the most functional people he could train for jobs, and was successfully getting them off the streets, long-term at times. Saving a dozen people from the streets per year was a big victory for him. And no question, saving one person is worthwhile. We were serving 250 to 300 a night, ten or twelve times a year, but admittedly not getting them off the streets. I pointed out to him once that his mission and mine were typical of a father and mother. He was urging them to get an education and a job; I was more concerned with keeping them warm, dry, well fed, and alive. In truth, they needed both of us.

Once I was clear about our mission, we began to hone in on what was needed to help people stay alive. Experience was our best teacher. The supplies we started out with were very basic, and sometimes it took a while for us to figure out what was most useful. The homeless themselves taught us. It was important to me from the beginning to give them clean, new, high-quality things. I didn't want to give them cast-offs, old clothes that didn't fit and were already worn or dirty, or poor-quality goods that would fall apart. We always gave away first-rate, durable supplies, which added immeasurably to our costs. The first thing we added, after the first miserable winter of driving rains, was a rain poncho. There was no point giving them warm jackets if they were going to be soaked to the skin shortly after, while their new jackets turned into sponges. A rain poncho seemed essential. One night, an older man asked if we had a warm scarf. That was an easy addition and made sense to us too. Jane, with her retailing experience, was extraordinary at finding the best quality and best deals, and ordering supplies.

We then ordered a waterproof tarp to cover the sleeping bags, and another to put underneath it. By then, our supplies were really all over the vans, and it was nearly impossible for us to find the bits and pieces—and even harder for someone to juggle it all as they walked back to their camps. It became clear to us that we needed a bag to carry it all when they left us. Jane found a good one, a big black nylon bag that held everything we gave them. A whole other team packed the bags on weekends in my garage.

In order to identify the size of the clothing in our bags, we tied yellow ribbons on the handles for medium, red for large, and blue for extra large. It made distributing the bags easier and more efficient. We had stopped ordering women's sizes by then—we saw too few women, and gave them the men's mediums instead. It worked. The bags were strong, serviceable, lightweight nylon. The color we ordered the first time, and stuck with thereafter, was black. Much of the time when people talked about us on the streets, they called us the "black bag people," and over time, we became legendary. It thrilled me whenever I saw our bags on the street, around town, being pushed on carts, which happened a lot.

In time, we added more and more items to the bags, all of which proved to be essential or at least useful for life on the streets. In addition to the warm down jackets, we added track suits, also warm, and also in three sizes like the jackets. Then we added long johns to go under the track suits. We were already giving out socks, gloves, wool beanies, and warm scarves. We researched shoes for a long time; sizes were a problem until we found an open sandal, which we bought in three sizes too. Hand warmers to slip into the gloves were a great addition and got good reviews from our clients. With the rain ponchos and waterproof tarps, we added umbrellas. We also added flashlights, notepads, and pens so they could leave messages for each other. We addressed these needs after talking to our clients. And we put in decks of cards for distraction. We put in a few small tools, like can openers, eating utensils, much later water bottles. And eventually, I realized that if any of our clients were fortunate enough to get a job interview, they had no way of cleaning up for it, so we began including hygiene supplies: combs, razors, mouthwash, toothbrushes, toothpaste, deodorant, wipes to clean their hands, shampoo, tampons. And as a quirk of my own, we added bars of really good soap. I like nice soap, and it seemed like a small luxury to offer them, instead of something more rudimentary. So within a relatively short time, with the contents of our bags, they were able to stay dry and warm, and get clean.

We had stayed away from offering them food for a long time. By distributing supplies to the homeless, we were breaking no laws. But the rules and laws about food are far more stringent. You need a license to serve or give out cooked or open food. And sadly, we learned that those laws were in place because now and then really twisted, malevolent people had poisoned homeless people with cooked food. Others had given them old food that was spoiled. So you were forbidden to give cooked or raw food to the homeless, in our city anyway. It had to be industrially packaged and sealed. Giving them food seemed complicated to me, since they had no opportunity to cook anything, warm it, or refrigerate it. Despite frequent requests, I didn't want to branch out into food. The big black bags were already chock full, and our budget stretched. But too often, our clients were asking if we had anything to eat, and looking disappointed when we didn't. So eventually, we began researching what food we could give them, and it turned out to be less complicated than I had feared.

The challenge was to figure out what was good to eat, nourishing, and didn't need to be cooked or refrigerated. We bought tins of tuna fish, chicken, Spam, and assorted meats that came in cans, with a can opener, of course. We included some tins of fruit. Instant powdered soups, instant hot cereals, which needed only to add hot water, which they could find. Cold cereals, peanut butter, jelly, crackers, potato chips, beans, beef jerky, nuts, dried fruits, Power Bars, cookies, chocolate, and coffee, tea, instant hot chocolate, sugar, and powdered cream. In time, we gave them packaged food that we calculated could last for about three weeks if used judiciously. And our clients were thrilled. It made the bags heavier—we had to order bigger bags once the food was added—but it met a very real need, and no one complained about how full the bags were. And if they were too heavy, for the women for instance, the men would help carry the bags back to their cribs or camps. The addition of the food was much appreciated by all.

We got requests for water too, but that was a problem we couldn't solve for them. Bottled water would have made the bags much too heavy, both for them and for us. Once the food was added, I already had a much harder time dragging the heavy bags out of the van, and bottled water would have made it impossible, for me and also for any of the women on the streets to carry. Although we were asked often for water, we just couldn't supply it. So instead we gave out an empty water bottle that they could fill on their own. It was the best we could do.

Another thing we decided not to supply was any kind of medication. Although many of the people we served on the streets were sick and needed treatment for both minor and major ailments, and cough and cold remedies would have been useful, I was afraid to give them anything that someone might be allergic to and inadvertently cause greater harm. I didn't want to take that risk. I also felt that giving medication might encourage them not to go to emergency rooms or clinics when they needed to, so we purposely didn't put them in. All we included were bandages and antiseptic.

People knew when we were on the streets. News traveled fast, and many people had figured out our schedule and roughly when we were due out again. We covered as large an area as possible, combing most of the places where the homeless hung out and lived. We asked people where others were camping, and went looking for them in grocery-store parking lots, back alleys, under overpasses, near construction sites, in places no one would suspect that people were hiding and living. As best we could, we found them. And a lot of them found us.

One of the more useful tools and means of communication on the streets are "cell phones," and not the kind you put in your pocket. In the language of the streets, a cell phone is a person on a bicycle who rides from one group to another, bringing news and linking people to what's happening nearby. Thanks to the "cell phones" cycling around the areas we worked in, a lot more people heard about us and came running. We were grateful for them, as they allowed us to reach out to so many more.

The number of bags we handed out rapidly jumped from 75 to 100, to 125 and then to 150. We'd been doing it for a while when we finally upped the numbers to 200, and then to 250, and on some nights 300. You didn't have to do anything to qualify for a bag. All you had to do was be there. People who said they needed another one for a husband, a wife, a girlfriend or boyfriend, or just a pal who was in his crib three blocks away and too sick to walk to us, were given the additional bag they said they needed. Who were we to question if what they said was true? Life was tough enough for them, without our making it more so. And to this day, I know and believe that in almost every instance, those bags were not sold to buy illegal substances or traded for them. Everyone we saw immediately opened the bags and put everything on, and ripped open the food bags with trembling hands. I saw many of those bags around the city, in the hands where they belonged, as people carried their possessions in them. For the most part, the bags stayed where they were meant to.

A Gift of Hope

Theft is a bigger problem on the streets, and too often people reported to us that they had been ripped off. I can't tell you how many times we went out and had people come running up to us in despair, saying their bag had been stolen only days before (or taken by the DPW and tossed in a garbage truck). "I knew you'd come back," more than one said to us. "I started praying for you to come this morning. Where were you? I needed a new bag.... Thank God, you made it." Providence seems to have shoved us out the door and onto the streets on the days we were most needed. And with impressive honesty, many times someone would shake their head with a smile, and say, "You got me last time, I'm okay ...." Or tell us they needed only a jacket but not a sleeping bag. Need is acute on the streets, but greed is rare, almost nonexistent. And time and time again, they wanted to make sure we gave something to their buddy, who they said needed it more.

I can't say I was never afraid as scary-looking people rushed toward us. I'm not crazy, and this was an unfamiliar world to me for a long time, full of people who at times could look ominous, disoriented, or even deranged. Sometimes they were less frightening when we started to talk to them, and at other times, they became considerably worse, and more alarming. In my earliest days on the streets, on a night when several very disturbing-looking people ran up to me, I pulled myself together and thought, *If Jesus came to me looking like this man, would I run? Or would I stand right where I am, face him, and embrace him?* I forced myself to see Jesus in him every time I saw someone who scared me, and eventually I felt blessed, not frightened. And the people who had seemed so upsetting to me melted into the kind people, who welcomed us into their world. That vision worked for me.

To remind myself of it, I bought a nearly life-size painting at an art fair. It was a painted cutout of a man, with the face of Jesus and a crown of barbed wire on his head, dressed in bright colors, holding a sign that says "Will work for food." It is unnervingly lifelike, and I put it on the wall outside my bedroom, where I can see it from my bed. Many times in the moonlight, I have jumped when I saw it, thinking there was a strange man standing outside my bedroom. And then I remember what it is, and what it was meant to remind me of. I love that painting, because it reminds me of the people I see on the streets and imagine with the face of Jesus, the people who no longer scare me. It is a constant reminder of the work we loved so much.

The sad thing is that we could have given away four or five times as many of our black bags on any given night. But buying adequate supplies for three hundred bags was expensive. We just couldn't give away more than that. I wish we could have, and still could.

The final thing we added to what we gave away was a crazy

idea I had one Christmas that turned out not to be so crazy after all. There is a child in all of us, who needs to be indulged occasionally, tended to, or at least acknowledged. But clearly, these people struggling to survive on the streets don't have time for childish pursuits. I have always had a fondness for teddy bears, and the comfort they represent. And teddy bears to me are also the spirit of Christmas. As disappointing as the holidays can be at times, there is still a child in each of us who hopes they will be different. And since our mission was one of hope, I wanted to add a teddy bear to the bags one Christmas. It brought up considerable debate among us. Was it a good idea? Wasn't it? Was it a waste of our money? Would anyone care, or even want them? And should we put a bear in each bag or hand them out separately? Most of the men on the team thought it should be put in the bag, to be discovered later. The women thought it should be handed out, which might be more personal and human. To be honest, even I thought that probably most of the teddy bears would wind up in a trash can or the gutter. Since 90 percent of our clients were men, and all of them were pretty rough, it was hard to imagine them seeing a teddy bear and not laughing in our faces. But I wanted to do it anyway. Something in my heart made me feel that it was a gesture they needed. And it meant a lot to me. I was willing to look foolish and at least try it.

On that particular Christmas, two wonderful ladies who

own a store donated three hundred small teddy bears; after that we bought them. But that first time was an experiment, and we all felt a little sheepish, but we bravely handed out a teddy bear, and said "Merry Christmas" or "Happy Holidays," to everyone who got a bag.

None of us was prepared for the reaction. The first man we handed it to must have been about six-four, a powerful man with unkempt hair, a somber face, and an aggressive expression. He looked at us, staring at the bear in his hand, and as I waited for him to throw it at me, instead he melted into tears as we looked at him in amazement. "Oh my God!" he said. "A teddy bear . . . I'm going to name him Oscar Junior the Second." Apparently, he himself was Oscar Junior. He thanked us profusely and walked off with his bag full of supplies in one hand, and the bear clutched to his chest with the other. It went like that all night—huge, tough-looking men, and it seemed like there were a lot of them that night, clutching their bears, naming them, holding them, and exclaiming in delight and astonishment. Some of them just stood there and cried as they held them. More predictably, the women loved them, and often cried too. But it was the men who undid us, who seemed to unravel in front of our eyes, softening visibly, and who loved them as much as did the women. Not a single person refused a teddy bear that night, and in the many years after, I don't think even five people refused them.

A Gift of Hope

We quickly figured out that we had hit on something important, and the bears were then included in every trip. No
one got a black bag without a teddy bear. The bears were
magic. Somehow, with that single gesture, we had restored
not only a memory of their childhood, but a tender part of
their humanity that had been missing. It wasn't just about
survival that night, clothing and feeding people and getting
them into warm clothes and a sleeping bag. It was about
touching a part of them that had been lost and forgotten.
They looked into the faces of those bears, and a piece of them
came back to life as they held their bears. It was one of the
most tender moments we had on the streets, and I was so
grateful that we had the bears to give. Some of our clients who
got bags on repeated trips had little bear families in their
shopping carts or their sleeping bags. The men weren't embarrassed to have them. Almost all the bears had names, and
were a piece of something they had found again and wanted
to hang on to. The bears became a tangible sign of the love we
all need and long for, a bridge from our hearts to theirs. I think
they became a symbol of all they had lost, forgotten, and
hoped to find again.

EIGHT

Other Groups and What They Do

Although what we did on the streets was unusual—there are so few outreach groups, and what we provided materially was unique—there are nonetheless some truly exceptional groups of people, serving the homeless population. Because federal, state, and city governments provide such inadequate help, and because severe budget cuts across the board have shut programs down, private citizens are doing what they can. Some of these groups have been in operation for as long as twenty years, and many of them have become established organizations and have achieved impressive results. Each organization has a different, specific focus, mission, and goal. They operate independently, and there is very little communication between the various groups. They are too busy helping people most of the time to talk to each other. A few years ago, I tried to organize a coalition among six of these groups, to share information and exchange ideas to better serve the homeless. It was amazing to me that due to lack of public effort, these groups had sprung up to meet a need that was not being met otherwise. The coalition was called Bridge of Hope. It eventually petered out, because the people involved were just too busy with their work on the streets to come to meetings. No one had enough time. The existing outreach teams serve as an example and a model for anyone who wants to help, and could easily be organized in other cities. The problem of homelessness is nationwide, and not specific to any city, or even any country anymore.

One of the most impressive organizations working with youth in San Francisco is Larkin Street Youth Services. They help young people from roughly ages eleven to twenty-four. They provide shelter, housing, medical care, a clinic and living facilities for young people with AIDS (sadly common because of drug use), counseling, job training and locating, education, clothing, and family reunification when reasonable. They have numerous programs and the rarest of all things, two outreach teams, one in vehicles and the other on foot, to make contact with young people on the streets and try to bring them in and help them get their lives together and get off the streets.

Another excellent group is At the Crossroads, conceived a dozen years ago by a young social worker, experienced with adolescents, who felt that existing programs weren't reaching homeless kids. They too have an outreach team that goes out on foot, carrying backpacks of minor supplies (usually in small bottles, like you'd find on airplanes or in hotels, small shampoos and mouthwashes that a kid can keep in a pocket or a bag and that the outreach worker can easily carry). They carry condoms and candy too. There's a multitude of things in those backpacks. Their real goal is to make contact and maintain it. They meet regularly with kids on an ongoing basis at fast-food restaurants or in doorways, determined to make a difference and help them get off the streets when they're ready. They consult with their clients for as many years as necessary, and their goal is to help them "lead amazing lives," not just lives of survival and subsistence. Their results over the years have been impressive.

A remarkable woman, a nurse, one of thirteen children herself from a huge family of Irish origin, has gone out on the streets for twenty years, offering prenatal care to women. Her efforts have become the Homeless Prenatal Program, which is now well established and has grown and broadened to help families and children. And it was all started by one dedicated woman, just as At the Crossroads was started by one very young social worker who thought he could do more by taking to the streets on his own with a backpack. In both cases, the organizations have grown in the past two decades and have helped countless people. They and people like them are the unsung heroes of the streets.

Street Outreach Services, also known as SOS, provides urgent medical care to the homeless in a mobile unit, bringing doctors and nurses to the streets in vans. Their assistance is invaluable in taking care of the most acute medical needs.

When I first started on the streets and long before, there was also a group of doctors working to offer wound care, also an acute need among the homeless. They recently disbanded after nearly twenty years, and some of them have gone to Philadelphia to do the same work in that city.

Sage, a much respected group, helps women in situations of exploitation and abuse. They do some outreach work on foot, to get in touch with women and help them. Once they make contact, they have an office where women can come for a variety of therapies and treatments.

Caduceus is a group of dedicated psychiatrists offering free psychiatric care on the streets (and also have an office now). At least two of their psychiatrists are Harvard trained, and the work they all do and their dedication are impressive.

All of the groups I've mentioned now have offices to see clients, but all of them began and have continued as outreach groups, whose main work is in the field, going out to those who need them, as we did.

Glide Memorial Church, in the heart of the Tenderloin, has

no outreach team, but if homeless people can get there, Glide provides them with the most remarkable assistance I've seen yet, with everything from three free hot meals a day, to drop-in medical and psychiatric clinics and care from concerned nurses and physicians, to job and vocational training for youth, housing for all ages, a program to finish high school and even get them into college, and day-care services for teen-agers with babies and for young children. They serve over a million free meals a year and run an amazing operation.

St. Anthony's dining room also offers free meals.

Each of these organizations is admirable for what they do, and they can also serve as inspiration and models for people who want to help the homeless in other cities.

Although homelessness is a world problem, some other countries have this situation under far better control. But each country handles it differently. Socialized medicine in Britain and France provides better and more accessible medical and psychiatric care, which gets a lot of people off the streets. In France, mobile units in trucks, ambulances, and cars bring serious medical care right into the streets. A private organization in Paris, called the Restaurant of the Heart, brings food in trucks and vans, and a Catholic group called Emmaus, organized by the late Abbé Pierre, provides not only centers offering medical and psychiatric care but facilities to do laundry, a place to stay, and cultural activities that restore dignity. They also have outreach teams that go out seven nights a week on foot, from ten P.M. to eight A.M. We all have much to learn from each other.

But there still isn't enough outreach in any city, as witnessed by the fact that we see so many people living on the street, homeless, in cities all over the world. No city is exempt anymore from the problem. There are homeless people now even in small towns. Clearly, we all have to work harder and join forces to find effective solutions to the problem of homelessness. But first and foremost, we have to care.

NINE

In Conclusion

None of us can change homelessness single-handedly. Even working together, it is a huge and complex problem that will take years to solve. More funding needs to be made available to programs and agencies assisting the homeless. Both in- and out-patient facilities need to be available for those who are mentally ill. If you want to help, you can find an established group that works with the homeless, and do it in a safe way.

One of the couples who left a lasting impression on me was two people we saw in a doorway late one winter night when it was raining hard. We were on our way back, at the end of a long night, with only two black bags in the back of one van. We were tired and cold but we saw the figures sitting in a doorway, so we stopped and hopped out. And as we approached, I saw a youngish man, probably in his thirties, in a T-shirt and jeans and rubber flip-flops, soaked to the skin. There was a young woman facing him as they sat on the pavement in the doorway. They had absolutely nothing—no blanket, no covering, no supplies, not even a piece of cardboard to sit on. The young woman was crying and shivering, and as we approached, we could hear him speaking softly to her. We saw him put his jacket around her shoulders, and with one hand he was stroking her hair. His voice was as gentle as a mother's as he told her everything would be all right as we approached, and she looked at him in despair. She was wearing his jacket and shivering, and he kept telling her it was going to be okay. She wore a skirt so wet it was plastered to her legs. I have never seen so much love between two people in my life, and he had just given her the last scrap of warmth he had, leaving him even colder as he held her gently in his arms.

He wasn't bemoaning their fate; he wasn't telling her how cold he was or that it was somehow her fault that they were there. He was reassuring and comforting her, and just plain loving her, as we walked up to them, carrying the last two bags. It was like walking into someone's bedroom. They looked up at us, and we explained what we had: warm, dry clothes, jackets, food, sleeping bags. They both cried then, and so did we, and he looked at her with a knowing smile, as though to say, "See, I told you it was going to be okay." Without planning it, we had proven him right. Something wonderful had just happened to them, and to us. Seeing that kind of love between two people is an incredible gift. I don't think I have ever seen a gentler man, or two more loving, grateful people.

They thanked us and we left them there, drying off, putting on warm clothes, setting down tarps, rolling out the sleeping bags, checking out the food. It wasn't a permanent solution for them, but it was a reminder that things could get better for them, and hopefully did. But even at their darkest moment, he was able to comfort her, and they were loving to each other. And at the moment they least expected it, a gift of hope appeared. I have never forgotten what I saw between them that night, just as I haven't forgotten the others. But that young couple defined love for me.

Whatever happens, I hope that you will continue to hold on to hope too. Even in our darkest moments, it is there. And in all its tenderness and beauty, even if hard to see sometimes, it is life's greatest gift: the gift of hope. A precious gift to share.

AFTERWORD

When I first wrote this book, our activities on the streets were in the present tense, but as I rewrote it and added to it, they gently slipped into the past tense, much to our chagrin, particularly since in a difficult economy, with poverty programs shutting down, the need to help the homeless is ever more acute.

I never tired of what we were doing, and I was in love with our mission on the streets, but it became financially unrealistic. The costs of our operation were just too high.

The sad reality is that we are currently not on the streets, handing out black bags, and I miss it terribly. My heart is still on those streets.

Because I was so anxious to maintain my anonymity, I was the sole source of funds for Yo! Angel! for all eleven years that we were active. And there is no question, supplying three or four thousand people a year with what we gave them was very costly. And serving fewer people, or giving them less, didn't seem to work.

I still have the dream of becoming active on the streets again. The team is still waiting and available, and I think we would all go out again in a minute. If we do so, having finally spoken up, I would seek funds from other sources to add to my contributions, and try to get discounts on the goods we buy. I think it would make a big difference, and perhaps make it possible again. The need is there, greater than ever.

For a short time, we tried serving fewer people, which only frustrated us and the people we served. Taking only a hundred bags out seemed so paltry. We were empty-handed in an hour, people were clamoring for more, and we left too many people unserved. It just didn't work, for them or us.

We still had a few bags left for a while, and I would stop and give them to people I saw on cold nights until they were gone. I spend time in France, and have done a few "runs" there with a friend. It was the same idea as Yo! Angel! in the beginning. We bought sleeping bags and warm jackets, wool hats and gloves, put them in a van, and distributed them on cold nights. The French homeless population has far better resources available to them for housing, medical care, and psychiatric support than the homeless in the States, but homelessness is a serious problem there too, and around the world.

For three years, I have chafed at no longer doing this work, and not being on the streets, and then remembered that I never intended to do it forever. Originally, we organized the trips one at a time, and then became addicted. It became "one more," just "one more time," and then finally a full-time operation, buying supplies, packing the bags, and delivering them on the streets on a regular schedule. But I never lost sight of the dangers. The only thing that frightened me every time was the possibility that someone on the team could get hurt, or worse. I never wanted that to happen, but it could have. Given what we did, and where we did it, the risk factor was constant and all too real. We talked about getting stabbed or shot sometimes, and then put it out of our minds and decided it was worth the risk. None of us wanted to stop. But perhaps Providence intervened here. Maybe we were meant to stop when we did, for whatever reason. Maybe the gift of working on the streets, and the many blessings we derived from it as individuals, was given to us for eleven years and no more. We weren't foolhardy, but the team was courageous. Maybe it was meant to end when it did, on a good note, and without harm coming to any of us.

The gift of hope passes from hand to hand, like a baton.

We're all in this together. Meeting the needs of others is humbling. And I think Albert Einstein had it right when he said, "The only life worth living is a life lived in service to others." May God bless you, and the people we serve.

With all my love,
Danielle Steel

ABOUT THE AUTHOR

DANIELLE STEEL has been hailed as one of the world's most popular authors, with over 600 million copies of her novels sold. Her many international best sellers include *The Sins of the Mother, Friends Forever, Betrayal, Hotel Vendôme, Happy Birthday, 44 Charles Street, Legacy,* and other highly acclaimed novels. She is also the author of *His Bright Light,* the story of her son Nick Traina's life and death.

Visit the Danielle Steel website at daniellesteel.com.

ABOUT THE TYPE

This book was set in Albertina, a typeface created by Dutch calligrapher and designer Chris Brand. His original drawings, based on calligraphic principles, were modified considerably to conform to the technological limitations of typesetting in the early 1960s. The development of digital technology later allowed Frank E. Blokland of the Dutch Type Library to restore the typeface to its creator's original intentions.

DISCARD